UNDERSTANDING
The Old Testament

The Rev. J. Stafford Wright, M.A. (Cantab)

Lamentations, Ezekiel, Daniel

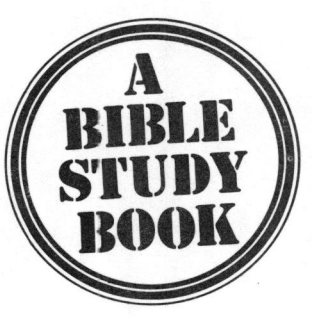

A BIBLE STUDY BOOK

Published in Great Britain by
Scripture Union
47 Marylebone Lane, London W1 6AX

© 1969 Scripture Union
First published 1969

Published as Daily Bible Commentary Vol. 2, 1977
Reprinted 1977
First published in this edition 1978

ISBN 0 85421 637 5

Printed and bound in Great Britain by
McCorquodale (Newton) Ltd, Newton-le-Willows

INTRODUCTION

Since their introduction, Scripture Union Bible Study Books have enjoyed wide popularity both in their original paperback and more recently as the hardback Daily Bible Commentary. The continued demand has led to their production in this new format. They are unique in that they can be used both as a daily Bible reading aid and as a complete commentary on the Old Testament.

A Daily Bible Reading Aid

Each volume is divided into sections of an appropriate length for daily use. Normally each volume provides material for one quarter's use, the exceptions being 1 Kings — Job (six months) Proverbs — Isaiah (six months) and Psalms (four months). Sections have not been dated but where it has been felt appropriate that two be read together in order to complete the book within a quarter they are marked with an asterisk.

A complete commentary of the Old Testament

Every major passage is expounded with devotional warmth, clear explanations and relevance to daily life. Most commentaries follow the rather artificial verse divisions, but here the writers have been commissioned to divide the material according to the best exegetical pattern. They thus follow natural units which allow the comments to follow more closely the flow of the original writers thought.

Writers have generally based their comments on the R.S.V. and readers will probably find this is the most suitable translation to use, although the comments will be found equally helpful with any other version.

Lamentations

The ascription of this Book to Jeremiah is not found in the Hebrew manuscripts, but first occurs in the Greek Septuagint translation after 200 B.C. Probably the collection of poems comes from more than one author, and Jeremiah could have been one of them. The acrostic style of writing strikes us as artificial, but form is no deterrent to reality, as with some of George Herbert's poems. The acrostic style here means that each verse, or group of verses, begins with a fresh letter of the alphabet, and works in order through all twenty-two letters. Psa. 119 similarly has an acrostic with eight verses to each letter. The metre, with a longer line balanced by a shorter to complete the sense, is known as the *qinah* metre, and it is used for funeral laments.

A lament of this kind is difficult to divide into sections, but roughly we may note: (*i*) The description of Jerusalem's present state and how it came about (1–7). Her allies have turned against her (2), her festivals have ceased (4), and she has no leaders (6). A further description of how her enemies treated her (7) is found in Obad. 10–14.

(*ii*) The reason is ultimately the sins of the people (8–16). We note that Jerusalem's cry to God not only appeals to His pity (9,11,16), but confesses her sins (14), and admits that her sufferings have come through the anger of the Lord (12). It is common to find v. 12 applied to Christ's sufferings on the cross, and the verse is certainly true of these, when Christ took our sins upon Himself; but in the context the reference is to Jerusalem bearing her own sins.

(*iii*) Submission to God's hand (17–22). Again there is the confession which admits that God is in the right (18). This is often a hard admission to make. One can feel the agony of heart that is wrung out even while the people make confession. Thus the verses combine the cry to God with further descriptions of the tragic state of the city and its people. The last two verses are a tentative prayer that God will vindicate His righteousness among the other nations. If Judah has needed to experience judgement to lead her to repentance, then others need the experience of judgement also.

As we read these laments, we may be enjoying all the comforts of home, and these descriptions seem rather remote. But some of our fellow Christians are suffering as Jerusalem suffered. We ourselves may also suffer various kinds of deprivation. Such suffering is always a call to heart-searching, but not all suffering is due to personal sin (e.g. 1 Pet. 5.6–11).

Compare this chapter with the parable of the prodigal son (Luke 15.11–32).

Lamentations 2   The Lord's Doing

This lament is largely a vivid description of what the writer sees and has seen. There are phrases that suggest that Jeremiah might well have written this Section before he was taken to Egypt. Note what is said about the false prophets (14, cf. Jer. 23.16,25), the law and the prophets, (9, cf. Jer. 18.18), and the phrase about terrors on every side (22), a favourite phrase of Jeremiah's (Jer. 6.25; 20.3,10; 49.29).

Moreover it would be like Jeremiah to declare repeatedly that it is the Lord who has brought all these tragedies upon Jerusalem (1–8), for he had frequently prophesied that the Lord would bring destruction on the city (e.g. Jer. 19.7–9). God has even destroyed that which, as it were, formed the base of His throne on earth, His footstool (1), which is either the ark with the mercy-seat upon it (1 Chron. **28**.2), or the whole Temple (Ezek. **43**.7; Pss. **99**.5; **132**.7). The author uses various pictures, including that of the booth of leaves and branches which sheltered the watchman when the fruit was ripening, and which was left to fall to pieces after the harvest (6, cf. Isa. **1**.8).

Next comes a description of people (9–17). Leaders have gone (9), old and young are helpless (10), and infants are starving (11,12). If only the prophets had spoken clearly about sin, as Jeremiah had done (14). Now the enemy imagine that they have scored over God in destroying the city (15,16), but they were only instruments in God's hands (17, cf. Isa. **9**.8–17).

The lament closes with a call to prayer (18–22). Nothing is said directly about repentance, but the whole tone of the chapter, which has admitted the hand of God, takes such repentance for granted. Surely the little children, on whom so much of the future depends, may look to God, when even their mothers cannot feed them (19), but actually murder them for food (20, cf. Jer. **19**.9).

A horrible description; but there are times when we must understand what suffering is.

Lamentations 3.1-33 Personal Tragedy

In this lament each letter of the alphabet occurs three times as the initial letter of a line, i.e. the Hebrew A is the first letter in vs. 1,2,3; B is the first letter in vs. 4,5,6, etc. The tone is personal, and the lament might easily be included among the *Psalms*, without a specific reference to the destruction of Jerusalem. Either the author speaks for himself, or he is the representative of the remains of the nation in their approach to God.

It is interesting to see that several often-quoted texts come in this chapter, especially in vs. 19–27, and 33. The language also reminds us of some of Job's words (e.g. Job **16**.6–17; **30**.16–23). There is also a superficial likeness to Job in that at first there is no confession of sin, although one assumes that the writer has passed through the experiences of chs. **1** and **2**, which clearly confess that the sins of the people have brought the heavy hand of God upon them. Probably a number of years have passed, and the author looks now for the fulfilment of the promises of restoration and renewal that were also given by Jeremiah and Ezekiel (e.g. Jer. **33**; Ezek. **36**). He is clearly a godly man, concerned to live to the glory of God. He prays that he may experience the mercy and compassion that are found in God.

With vivid pictures he describes the tragedy of his present existence (1–18). Then he turns his eyes from self to God (19–33). We note the great covenant word which the RSV regularly translates as 'steadfast love' (22). The covenant is a powerful plea, as in the claiming of the Davidic covenant in Psa. **89,** which in vs. 38–45 again reminds us of this lament. The covenant can never be presumed upon, but the author here truly casts himself on God as his only 'portion' ('allotted share', Moffatt), is prepared to wait for Him, and to work out lessons of disciplined patience that he has learned while he was young (24–30). He knows that God does not torment mankind for the joy of seeing them suffer (33).

We often need patience, cf. Heb. 10.35–38: Jas. 5.11.

Lamentations 3.34-66   Prayer in the Dark

We noticed that at first there was no confession of sins. Now the speaker remembers all the oppression of which the prophets had spoken (34–36), and declares that this is one reason why the Lord came down in judgement (38). *Good* and *evil* here mean God's hand in history in blessing and calamity (cf. Zeph. 1.12). There are other sins also, and we must examine ourselves in the sight of God, and not only examine, but repent and turn back to God (39–42). Sin has put a dark cloud between God and man, and now we seem to be praying still in the dark (43–45).

The writer becomes freshly aware of his enemies, who were glad to see Judah and its peoples, including the writer, brought low (46–51). Vs. 52–57 clearly speak of persecution, but it seems as though we have picture language rather than a literal description. One is reminded of Jeremiah in the dungeon pit, but vs. 53 and 54 were not literally true of his experience (Jer. 38.6–13). Similar picture language occurs in Psa. **40.**1–3.

In vs. 58–66 the writer sees by faith that God is intervening to vindicate His servant, or servants. This leads him to take the position which Jeremiah took in several of his prayers, when he saw that his enemies were God's enemies, since he was being attacked because he was true to the message that God gave him (e.g. Jer. **11.**18–20; **17.**14–18). The author of this lament does not go as far as Jeremiah, since he was not being persecuted for his faith, but the enemy, in their treatment of Judah, were going far beyond what God would have had them do as His instruments (cf. Zech. **1.**15). So, while he does not pray for their destruction, he asserts that God will hold them guilty for what they are doing while they hold the land in occupation (64–66).

Peoples without God's revelation through His written Word are responsible to Him for acts of atrocity that shock the human conscience (cf. Amos I).

Lamentations 4

In this lament an eye-witness has given one of the most vivid pictures that we have of a conquered city. He presents themes that we have already seen, especially in ch. 2, but in an even more moving way. There is no reason why Jeremiah should not be the author, although in v. 20 he seems to commend king Zedekiah instead of condemning him as he did in his prophecies. But in v. 20 he describes the king as the people hopefully saw him at his coronation.

Try to soak in the pictures of Zion, comparing them with ruined or bombed buildings that you know, and visualizing the state of the people in the light of horror pictures of suffering peoples today. Read of the debris blocking the streets (1); of people as they were before the disaster and as they are now (2,5,8); of mothers unable to feed their starving children (3,4); of the horrors of cannibalism, when suffering has killed the finer feelings (10); of good-looking men whose faces are pinched and unrecognizable (7,8), and who are thankful to find a home in a rubbish dump (5); of crops pillaged by the invaders (9).

Sometimes we can see no reason at all for a nation's sufferings, but the people of this nation know that their wrongdoing had brought a seemingly impregnable city to the ground (11,12). The religious leaders had backed the cruelties that meant persecution, conviction, and death for the innocent, who had land or property that could be seized (13, e.g. Isa. 1.15; Jer. 2.34). But when Jerusalem was captured, those prophets and priests that escaped were so battered and wounded that no nation would receive them, recognizing them as being far from holy men (14,15), which indeed is how God Himself regarded them (16).

Now we are taken back to memories of the fall of the city. There was a vain and persistent hope that the Egyptians would come to the rescue (17; Jer. 37.5–10; Ezek. 29.6,7). The tall Babylonian siege towers made it dangerous for anyone to walk in the streets within range of arrows or stones (18). Then came the fall of the city, and the break-out (19; Jer. 39.4,5), with the capture of Zedekiah as he tried to cross the Jordan to safety (20). There is little doubt that the Edomites, who knew the routes and crossings, helped the Babylonians here, and this is why vs. 21,22 turn against Edom. Obad. 14 clearly shows what they did. So, when Zion is restored, Edom will still be kept low, and Mal. 1.2–5 records that this was fulfilled. Ultimately Edom was subdued and absorbed into Israel (see notes on Ezek. 35).

Pray for those who are being driven to believe that they were better dead (9).

Although this lament has twenty-two verses, it is not an acrostic. It is, however, an equally vivid eye-witness picture to what we had in ch. **4**. So again we have scope to let the picture sink in, and remember that these horrors still haunt the world in one part or another.

We cannot tell how long these conditions lasted, but the probability is that the land in general was occupied by Edomites and others, who took steps to see that Jerusalem was not rebuilt, and that the Jews themselves, who had not been taken to Babylon, should be exploited to the utmost (Ezek. **36.**1–7).

The reference to Assyria in v. **6** is difficult, since she had long ceased to be an empire, although Egypt was a place to which refugees had gone (Jer. **43**). Perhaps the verse is a condensed allusion to former alliances with Assyria and Egypt that the prophets had denounced (2 Kings **16.**7–9; Isa.**7.**1–9; **30.**1–7), i.e. once our fathers looked to them for grand military help; now we should be thankful if they would give us enough employment to supply the bare necessities of life.

The result of the sins of the fathers is truly stated (7), but it is not the whole truth if (as Ezekiel shows in **18.**1 ff) it becomes an excuse for sitting down passively. The description continues, with former slaves ingratiating themselves with the occupying nations (8), and with crops seized in sudden raids (9). Good native leaders are dealt with by arrest and torture (12). Press gangs take the young away (13) and the old have no heart for free speech in meetings at the city gates (14), and there is no more music and dancing (14,15). We are like dethroned kings (16).

We cannot only blame our fathers, but we ourselves are involved in guilt, and are morally, spiritually, and physically sick (16,17, cf. Isa. **1.**5,6; Jer. **8.**22; **17.**9). As the writer looks at the ruins of Zion (18), he lifts his eyes to the eternal God (19, cf. Heb. **1.**8). Restoration cannot be only from rubble to reconstruction, but must be from a self-directed life to God Himself at the centre (21).

Which prayer must ultimately take priority: 'Restore me to my . . .' (we can fill in the blank); or, 'Restore me to Thyself'? (cf. 2 Cor. 12.8–10).

Questions for further study and discussion on Lamentations

1. Is there any value in taking a straight look at our sufferings?
2. How far does *Lamentations* keep a balance between looking at ourselves and looking to God?

3. Is all suffering deserved? Can we pass judgement on individual cases?
4. At what point can a Christian pass from confession to claiming the promises of God?
5. If you are interested in questions of authorship, consider whether Jeremiah may reasonably be suggested as the author of any or all of these laments. Note that the ascription to Jeremiah is only traditional, but tradition generally contains some truth.

Ezekiel

INTRODUCTION

Ezekiel was a Jewish exile in Babylonia. He was taken captive with the young king, Jehoiachin, in 597 B.C., and there is no indication that he ever returned to live in Judah. He was called to be a prophet about 593 B.C. Jerusalem was still intact, since the next siege and destruction of the city was in 588–7 B.C. There were so-called prophets in Jerusalem and Babylonia who were declaring that the Jehoiachin captives would soon return (Jer. 28.1–4; 29. 15–28). Jeremiah in Jerusalem and Ezekiel in Babylonia both announced the doom of Jerusalem and a further captivity unless the people really repented. Yet both prophets were shown that there would eventually be a return and Jerusalem would be rebuilt, but this would be accompanied by repentance and renewal.

Roughly speaking the *Book of Ezekiel* may be divided into three sections according to subject matter:

1–24 The doom of the rebellious nation.
25–32 God's verdict on some other nations.
33–48 The restoration and renewal of Judah and Israel.

Ezekiel 1.1-14   Visions in Exile

The setting is Babylonia in a Jewish settlement by the large canal, Kabaru, which formed an eastern loop in the Euphrates from above Babylon to Uruk (Erech) via Nippur (1). Ezekiel was living there as one of the exiles taken with King Jehoiachin in 597 B.C. (2; 2 Kings 24.8–16). He was a priest, but we have no

9

other record of his father, Buzi (2). If the reference in v. 1 is to his age, this would coincide with the time that he would probably have entered on his full service of priesthood at the age of 30 had he remained in Jerusalem. (N.B. Levites in Num. 4.3, and Jesus Christ in Luke 3.23).

Although he could not act as priest, God called him as prophet. Ezekiel here and elsewhere describes the experience of inspiration as being seized by the hand of God (3; 3.14,22; 8.1, etc., cf. 1 Kings 18.46; Isa. 8.11; Jer. 1.9). The result here is an amazing vision of God. In reading it we realize that Ezekiel is struggling to convey the indescribable. Notice his use of such phrases as 'the likeness of', 'something that looked like', 'the appearance of'.

The visionary appearance of God comes in a storm cloud, (Job 37.22–38.1) from the north, the direction in which one would normally go to Jerusalem from Babylon via the Fertile Crescent. The cloud flashes fire (Exod. 19.16), and unfolds to disclose its source in a centre like dazzling reflecting metal (4). From the cloud come four living creatures. Later Ezekiel refers to them as cherubim (ch. 10), and John also sees them around the throne of God in Rev. 4.6,7. Some have found a symbolic meaning in their four faces as representing aspects of created life (10), but they may well be angelic attendants of the throne of God, depicted as Ezekiel and John saw them, just as Isaiah describes them as seraphim (Isa. 6.2).

Their four faces look in four directions with each human face looking outwards (10). Their legs and hands are of human type (7,8), though instead of human feet they apparently have something like a rounded hoof (7). Today Ezekiel might have described them as castors, the point being that they could move instantly in any direction (9,12). They each have four wings; one pair covers their bodies, the other pair extends straight from their shoulders so as to touch the tip of their neighbour's wings (11). They thus form a square, living and instantly mobile (14), and later we find that they are supporting the visionary throne of God. Meanwhile Ezekiel sees fire at the centre of the square, probably now as an altar fire from which torches are kindled (13, cf. Isa. 6.6).

God's servants are able to go where His Spirit wishes them to be (12; Rom. 8.14).

Ezekiel 1.15-28 Visions of God

As the vision unfolds it is seen that the four cherubim form part of a chariot. Although this has four wheels, one under each cherub, and thus centralized, each wheel is composed of two wheels apparently at right angles to each other. This is impossible in reality, but in the vision it enables the chariot to run instantly in any direction without turning (16,17). The wheels shine like yellow quartz (16), but they are not dead metal; their livingness is shown by their eyes with which they can see the way (18, cf. Rev. 4.8), and by their life-link with the living creatures above them (20,21).

The significance of the vision unfolds further: it is not simply an interesting glimpse of angelic beings. Now Ezekiel sees a gleaming crystal platform over their heads (22). Next he notices the wings extended in motion and lowered when at rest. In the speed of movement their wings roar in the air like a waterfall or thunder (23,24). Then comes a sudden silence as their wings are lowered and the chariot stops, and Ezekiel hears a voice from above (25).

This leads to the culmination of the vision, the gloriously bright figure of God, in appearance like a man, enthroned on the crystal platform. The description suggests that Ezekiel did not see a face and body that he could have drawn, but rather a fiery brightness that had a human shape and that he knew to be living and personal. Note his careful use of words, 'the appearance of the likeness of the glory of the LORD' (28). No one in O.T. times saw God in His full Being (John 1.18. N.B. John was well aware of O.T. appearances of God). But from time to time God revealed Himself in a selected form. Many believe that such visions were pre-incarnation appearances of Jesus Christ, as John 12.41 suggests in the context which refers to Isa. 6. Such appearances could illuminate, but could not redeem: for redemption full Incarnation was necessary, and not simply an appearance as a Man.

God above the cherubim is not confined in the Temple (Exod. 25.22; 2 Kings 19.15), nor anywhere else (Psa. 18.10; John 4.21–24).

Ezekiel 2.1—3.3   Message Received

The title 'Son of man' (1) occurs some 90 times in this book. It is a Hebraism which is an emphatic form of 'man'. It probably reminds Ezekiel, that in comparison with the majesty of God, he is merely mortal man. We still need this reminder, which is not inconsistent with the love of God. Ezekiel's attitude and God's call to him to rise should be compared with Dan. 10.9,10 and Acts 26.14–16.

There are a number of references to the Spirit in *Ezekiel*; these should be noted as they occur, and might well now be scanned in a concordance. We have already had a specialized reference in 1.12,20,21. Now the Spirit is the inspirer of the prophetic word, who enters into Ezekiel (2).

Note how Isaiah (**6.**9–12), Jeremiah (**1.**17–19) and Ezekiel, here (**3**–**7**), were all given a depressing call. They were needed in a desperate situation, and had to be prepared for a large measure of rejection and even threats on their life. There is always a mystery about preaching and speaking the Word of God. It may be law, love, or threat—all three are the Word of God—but experience shows that many who hear will reject.

We must, however, be convinced that the message is truly God's. A prophet was always confident that God had given him His true Word. Thus Jeremiah had God's words put into his mouth (**1.**9), and Ezekiel here is given a written scroll to digest. It is the objective Word of God which becomes part of himself. That is why we study the Bible and do not merely skim through it. The words that Ezekiel was to utter at this stage in his ministry were of gloomy tragedy (10), but in so far as they were God's words for him they were as sweet as honey (**3.**3). When John was given a similar scroll in Rev. **10.**8–11 it also was sweet to the taste, but was bitter to his digestion. How enthusiastic we are when we suddenly see the glory of the gospel that God has given us to pass on! How bitter we find it when we are faced with the rejection of what means so much to us! (Jer. **15.**16–18).

If even Christ's preaching 'failed' (Luke 13.34), what hope is there for our witness (1 Cor. 9.22)?

Ezekiel 3.4-15 People Next Door

Ezekiel had the hardest commission of all—to witness to his next-door neighbours. People with prophetic or pseudo-prophetic gifts were regarded with awe in countries beyond their own, e.g. Elisha (2 Kings **5** and **8.**7–9), Jeremiah (**39.**11–14) and Jonah (**3.**6–10). Ezekiel might have traded on this, and had a more encouraging life (5,6). We must take this into account in weighing up a possible missionary call.

Verse 7 is one of the most dangerous verses in Scripture, though the Bible does not hesitate to include it, and indeed, there is a similar sentiment in the N.T. (Luke **10.**16). It is a call to intense humility, for fear that we comfort ourselves concerning our off-putting presentation of the truth by calling our rejection the rejection of Christ. Off-putting presentation can lie in our own character as well as in inept words out of season. Yet v. 7 must at times bring comfort to the true Christian who burns to see others won.

This may demand a certain toughness (8,9). Again, these verses can be dangerous if they are taken out of the context of the whole

12

Bible. We must seek the power of the Spirit to make us less personally sensitive, while remaining lovingly sensitive to the needs around
us. Distinguish Christ's toughness towards the hard religious
leaders from His tenderness towards the outcasts of society.

One cure for a wrong attitude is the preliminary application of the
Word of God to ourselves (10). Let what we hear with our ears go
deeply into our hearts (Matt. 13.23). Then go out with God's
message.

When Ezekiel was inspired as a prophet, he had strange experiences.
Like the Lord Jesus he felt himself driven by the Spirit (Mark 1.12).
Already the honeysweet Word had become bitter (14) as he strode
down the banks of the canal to the exile settlement at Telabib. He
knew the general drift of the Lord's will, but for seven days he
waited until the actual word for the moment was given to him.

Consider Luke 4.24.

Ezekiel 3.16-21   Watchman's Warning

A prophet knew the difference between his own thinking and the
Word of the Lord that laid hold of him. Here v. 16 may be compared with Jer. 42.7. Ezekiel has to see himself as a watchman on
sentry-duty to warn the people of the city (17, cf. Jer. 6.17; Hab.
2.1). The trouble is that the people may be too sleepy or too busy
to take the warning when it comes (Luke 21.34).

This is one of the passages in Scripture that links sin and death.
It is not always easy to know whether the reference is to the death of
the body or to the eternal death. Physical death for human beings
comes because of sin (Rom. 5.12), but it also signifies death on a
further level, the death of the personality separated from the life
of God. So the Christian passes from death to life through living
faith in Christ, having his sins taken away through the work of
Christ (John 5.24). But unless he lives until the second coming of
Christ, his body will die, since death, having entered in, still operates
in the material world (1 Cor. 15.26). But this death of the body will
be reversed at the Second Coming and the resurrection. With
renewed bodies, after the pattern of Christ's risen body, we shall be
complete men and women through all eternity.

The warning in vs. 18-21 is to repent and turn from our wicked
ways, since these are ways of death. The verses have their fullest
meaning when applied to eternal death, though violent death sometimes comes as a sequel to an evil life. This could be the thought of
v. 20. The stumbling-block may be a disaster which God brings.
We are not concerned here with the N.T. teaching of eternal

13

salvation in Christ, but we see that even a good man, with a wealth of good actions behind him, may sink to the lower levels of world-behaviour. The N.T. shows that sometimes God allows premature death for such a person so as to cut him off from further wrongdoing (1 Cor. 5.5). If only he (and we) had responded to the watchman's warning!

Meanwhile we have responsibilities both as Christian watchmen and as citizens who need to hear the watchman's voice.

Study: Contrast this passage with Isa. 56.10–12.

Ezekiel 3.22-27 Kept Back

We have been a long time over preliminaries. Ezekiel is still waiting for the moment when the Word of God will come to him for the people. Probably he still needed personal preparation, so that he would see his calling more clearly. It was not sufficient to be a mechanical talking computer. His inner life must be true to the God-given message, and he must know the greatness of his responsibility.

First he has a renewed vision of the glory of the Lord (22,23). Already, perhaps, he had begun to turn in on himself under the strain that he could foresee was coming. A wise man once said something to the effect that we should take ten looks at Christ to one at ourselves.

Surely the time has now come to speak! Yet surprisingly Ezekiel is ordered to shut himself in his own house. The probable meaning of v. 25 is that God will restrain him as though he were tied with ropes (cf. 4.8), though some interpret the verse to mean that his opponents will tie him up to prevent him from prophesying. The former meaning links well with v. 26, which again describes an act of God. Not only would Ezekiel be restrained from leaving home, but he would be totally unable to speak at all until the moment arrived to give the Lord's message.

The situation is puzzling at first sight. In the previous portion we saw the urgency to speak as a watchman because the people were rebellious. Now Ezekiel has to be silent because they are rebellious. The answer probably can be seen from the varied responses of people to the presence and talk of Christians. There is a place for talking about Christ and a place for quiet assurance that refuses to argue. No doubt a rumour had gone around that Ezekiel had been called to be a prophet. People came along out of curiosity (33.30–33), but found Ezekiel unmoving and silent in his house. This exasperated them and roused their curiosity for the message when it came. Yet in his silence Ezekiel was seeing his people with fresh eyes. He was ready for the Word to fall.

Consider occasions of silence in Pss. 4.4; 62.1; Matt. 26.63; John 8.6; 19.9.

Ezekiel 4.1-8 Serious Play

To act the siege of a city with the aid of a picture and imitation 'guns' sounds like a children's game. But prophets were often told to drive home their message by strange acted parables (e.g. Isa. 20.2,3; Jer. 13.1–7). The Jews were thinking of restoration rather than the destruction of Jerusalem, and certainly they did not suppose that, if a new attack came, God (as represented here by His prophet) would cut Himself off by an iron wall (3).

While he conducts the siege Ezekiel has to lie on his left side for 390 days and on his right for 40 days. There are three problems here:

(*i*) Did he lie for the whole period without moving? On physical grounds this is unlikely. Probably he lay like this during the hours when he was acting as prophet, and at other times behaved normally. There was no point in acting a parable with no one present to learn from it.

(*ii*) The period between Ezekiel's call (1.1,2) and his next dated utterance in 8.1 is one year and one month. We are not certain what calendar Ezekiel follows, but the period would be near enough to 390 days. To add another 40 would be too much. Probably for 40 out of the 390 days Ezekiel would turn over after completing the left side sign. The Greek Septuagint has 190 days, in which case the periods could be consecutive.

(*iii*) Commentators differ over the application of the numbers. Ezekiel could be reckoning from 922 B.C. when the northern kingdom of Israel split off in rebellion after the death of Solomon and made the golden calves (1 Kings 12). The round figure of 390 (a day for a year) brings us to 532 B.C. Babylon fell in 539 B.C., and the exiles were free to return in 538 B.C. If the Septuagint is correct, the date begins with the fall of Samaria and exile of the northern kingdom (722 B.C.) and takes us to 532 B.C., as before.

The 40 years for Judah date from the coming fall of Jerusalem in 587 B.C. Here again we must regard 40 as a round number, which has a symbolic significance as being the time of wandering in the wilderness before the first entry into Palestine. Yet by 547 B.C. Cyrus was already threatening the power of Babylon.

Consider the place of symbols in conveying truth, e.g. Sacraments.

15

By his signs Ezekiel was told to drive home the horrors of the coming siege of Jerusalem. In a sense he is called to identify himself with the sufferers. His food is to be coarse and scanty; plain bread and vegetables weighing about half a pound a day. Be realistic. If you cannot visualize this, weigh some bread on the kitchen scales. Ezekiel ate one meal a day, a famine meal every time. Some Christians wish to identify themselves with their brothers in need in the same sort of way as Ezekiel, and at the same time send them the cost that they save. Ezekiel was allowed two pints of water daily, but this had to be exactly measured out as though it were rationed (11,16).

Then came the order to use human excrement as fuel for cooking. Ezekiel took the lesson, but refused the action. As a priest he had always kept the Mosaic laws of cleanness and uncleanness. Although in v. 14 he refers to the general laws of uncleanness (e.g. Exod. 22.31), he must have had Deut. 23.13 also in mind. Most of the laws of hygiene in the Pentateuch make obviously good sense, and even those which are obscure undoubtedly have some reason that was valid under more primitive conditions.

God shocked Ezekiel into feeling the horror of exile in lands that were unclean (13). They were unclean because their religion and morals contained so much that attracted and yet contaminated. It is true that in the Holy Land the people of God had admitted any number of unholy Canaanite ways, but at least it was their land and they could reject them. As a minority in a foreign land they would have to bow to the will of the majority, and put up with things that horrified them if they cared for the true God at all.

Dried animal dung was used as fuel in the east, and still is, and it was not regarded as ritually unclean. However, in the siege all cattle would be killed for food, so only human excrement would be available for fuel.

Note how ancient is the expression of bread as the staff of life (16; Lev. 26.26; Psa. 105.16; Isa. 3.1; Ezek. 14.13).

To learn sympathy we must learn to share (1 Pet. 5.9).

Ezekiel 5   God the Enemy

This chapter is the completion of the signs in ch. 4, as is shown by v. 2. Shaving the head and beard was a sign of mourning (Isa. 22.12; Jer. 41.5). Ezekiel's first action shows that mourning would come through the sword of invasion. Afterwards, the hair itself represents the people, one part destroyed in the city, one part in battle, and one part blown into exile. Even some of the last group must be thrown into the fire, and the meaning of v. 4 may be that the wind blows them away burning. Thus the exiles already in Babylon would have an influx of fresh exiles still ablaze with their wickedness (cf. **14**.22,23).

Jerusalem, the chosen city, was the spiritual centre of the earth (5) and, indeed, of the universe, since Jesus Christ died there (Col. **1**.20). Yet her people had adopted lower moral standards than the unenlightened pagans (6; Rom. **2**.13–16) while substituting what was obviously wrong in paganism for the revealed standards of God (7, cf. 1 Cor. **3**.3; Gal. **5**.19–21).

From v. 8 onwards note the number of times when God says what 'I will' do. Here was the tragedy. They had turned God into their enemy. The destruction of Jerusalem is never regarded in the Bible as a chance event. Whether or not we choose to refer to the hand of God, history shows that moral degradation in various forms has resulted in the collapse of kingdoms and empires.

Note the accusation of defiling God's sanctuary (11). We shall read more of this in ch. 8. Meanwhile we can read 1 Cor. 3.16,17; 6.19,20, and take Ezekiel's lesson.

The strong language of v. 13 sounds shocking, but forms part of the whole picture. The Lord has told Ezekiel to act out a siege in which God Himself is the King who marches against a rebel city. Only when the city is subdued or destroyed is the King satisfied. The next siege of Jerusalem will be like that. The evil is so great that God cannot stop half-way. Otherwise what opinion would other nations form of His standards? We shall see the reverse picture in **36**.19–21.

*Study: It is worth comparing what God says here with what He said through Moses in Lev. **26**. There are some similar phrases.*

Questions for further study and discussion on Ezekiel chs. 1—5

1. Compare the calls of Ezekiel, Isaiah (ch. **6**), Jeremiah (ch. **1**), Moses (Exod. **3**).
2. Compare Ezekiel's opening vision with Rev. **4** and **5**.
3. What passages indicate that Ezekiel was more than God's typewriter?
4. Why should God be concerned about the behaviour of Jerusalem?

Ezekiel 6   Glamorous Religion

In reading the O.T. we must all the time be alive to metaphors and allusions, or we shall not make sense of the words. Thus God is not angry with the mountains (2) any more than with the cedars and oaks in Isa. 2.13,14. Probably in any part of Palestine at this time you would have found some mountain or hill crowned with an altar, one or two standing stones, a wooden pillar, and a clump of evergreen trees (Jer. 3.6–9). They were flourishing centres of the old Canaanite religion which should have been destroyed (Deut. 7.5). It is likely that some of the Jews and Israelites deceived themselves into thinking that they were worshipping Jehovah there: the local god went by the name of Baal, and this could mean 'lord' or 'master'; so why not apply it to Jehovah (cf. Hos. 2.16)? Others made no pretence about it. Jehovah was the God for special occasions at Jerusalem, but one had better keep on good terms with the local gods and goddesses as well, especially as the form of worship was sensual and exciting. This problem confronts Christians in some of the newer churches overseas. In civilized countries there are other substitutes.

There must have been some similar worship in the ravines and valleys (3; Isa. 57.5,6; Jer. 2.23; 7.31), perhaps sometimes cave worship of an earth-mother, or, as Isaiah and Jeremiah suggest, child sacrifice.

Now Ezekiel declares the helplessness of these nature gods and goddesses. Their worshippers run to their altars for sanctuary, and are killed and left to rot in the ruins (4,5). In a sense, they themselves become sacrifices. Certainly this is what Jeremiah was saying to the people in Jerusalem (Jer. 7.31–8.2).

The tragedy was that less than 30 years earlier King Josiah had been through the land destroying the centres of degraded worship (2 Kings 23.4–20), but this is the sad history that has been repeated again and again—enthusiasm, reform, coolness, relapse. Yet relapse may be followed by repentance, and this is the theme of vs. 8–10. The immediate prospect is terrifying, with the land devastated from south to north (11–14).

Read one of the Letters to the Seven Churches, e.g. Rev. 2.19–29.

Ezekiel 7.1-13 Doomsday

Here is a final cry of doom. Note the repetition of 'has come', applied to 'the end' (2,6), 'doom' (7,10), 'the time' (7,12), 'the day' (10,12). One really needs to read this aloud to get the full horror as Ezekiel's audience must have heard it. There are turning-points in history where we see a people brought to judgement. Because we are all so closely bound together, the innocent suffer with the guilty, but the innocent may see the rottenness of the whole body and make their protest for as long as they possibly can.

Ezekiel sees the movement of God against Judah's 'ways' and 'abominations' (3,4,8,9). The religious abominations were mentioned in 6.1–7 and will appear again in ch. 8. In estimating God's verdict we must remember that Israel was intended to mirror God's Person to the nations. When the mirror reflected the most superstitious and degraded religious practices in existence, it had to be broken, mended, and redirected.

The 'ways' were ways of antisocial behaviour, much as the prophets continually castigated (10,11). There had been far too much violence and injustice from the time of Solomon onwards (e.g. Isa. 5). Countries rising to independence, and to the opportunities of money and power, have to fight the same problems. In England we have the phrase 'I'm all right, Jack', meaning that I must look after myself irrespective of other people's needs and feelings. The business world offers severe temptations to ruthlessness. 'The day' can wreck the Stock Market as well as impoverish a country.

On Ezekiel's lips vs. 12 and 13 presumably mean that the devastation of the land will rob buyer and seller of their property, but the exact interpretation is difficult. Perhaps we may paraphrase: The purchaser must not rejoice at getting a bargain, nor must the seller regret having to part with his property, since he will not be there to watch another man occupying it: purchaser, seller, and indeed the whole nation, will be broken up in exile or death.

Consider permanent values, e.g. Matt. 6.19–21; 1 Cor. 3.11–15. (Note 'The Day'.)

Ezekiel 7.14-27   Unreliable Standards

The situation foretold in this section is reflected later in *Lamentations*. Meanwhile the picture unfolds as the gradual breakdown of all the 'securities' of life. This is the sort of thing that under the providence of God may pave the way for a genuine conversion today. Or it may lead to a sense of frustration and hollowness.

The challenge comes, but we have deteriorated too much to be free to meet it (14; John 8.34). The outlook is hopeless wherever we turn (15). We begin to be aware not only of our helplessness, but of our sin (16,17; Rom. 7.24,25). We repent in shame (18; 2 Cor. 7.10). We realize that our values are worthless under test. There are permanent things that money cannot buy, and we cannot eat money (or houses or television sets) when what we need is food to keep us from starvation (19; Psa. 49.6,7).

For many people in Judah money had been a stumbling-block of iniquity, that is, they had tripped over it and gone headlong into the bog, or into the animal pit (19). We have often joined in prayers for the needs of the poor. If the Bible is correct, the very rich need our prayers just as much as the very poor (Matt. **19**.22–24; 1 Tim. **6**.17–19).

The particular stumbling-block here is the use of silver and gold to make idols (20), and idols are substitutes for the true God. For us a God-substitute may be expensive or fairly cheap. In equating covetousness with idolatry (Col. **3**.5), the N.T. shows how wide an application this word has. In history a rich church has suffered at the hands of a greedy or needy world (21–23).

At another level unchecked violence breeds more violence, and trigger-happy aggressive nations, companies, or individuals, must not be surprised if they are one day cornered themselves (23–25).

There was a time when God's people could have enjoyed the Word of God, and the sane advice of wise men (26), and had a good and stable government (27). But the prophets and priests lost touch with the Word, and the ruling classes drifted into standards that made for destruction rather than stability (Jer. **5**.27–31).

Thought: 'I'm terribly sorry for Mr. . . . ; he has such a lot of money.'

Ezekiel 8.1-6 Image or Glory

Ezekiel is transported from Babylon to Jerusalem. He describes the sensation in v. 3. We are naturally curious to know 'how it was done', but the only clue is that it was an extension of a simple vision, and that its originator was the Spirit of God. It is unlikely that his body vanished from the sight of the elders (1). We can find a partial parallel in well-authenticated telepathic experiences, in which someone has 'seen' an event happening at a distance. The pictures that Ezekiel sees are partly real and partly symbolic.

This was not natural telepathy, but a special divine communication, introduced by the appearance of the Lord whom he had seen in his opening vision (2, cf. **1**.26,27). When the Lord touched him, the Spirit enlightened him (cf. the association of the prophet and the Spirit in Rev. **1**.10–16; **4**.1,2).

Ezekiel became, as it were, God's television screen, so that the exiles might see for themselves the utter degradation of Jerusalem, and thus understand why it had to be judged so drastically.

The Temple and the open-air altar of burnt offering were surrounded by a rectangular court. There was a gate in the north wall of the court opposite the altar. Ezekiel was set down by this gateway, probably just outside it. He faces north, away from the

Temple court, and looks across the next court to another gateway in which stood 'the image of jealousy' (3).

The word 'image' is *semel*, which occurs elsewhere only in Deut. **4**.16 (where it is translated 'figure') and in 2 Chron. **33**.7,15, of a special 'idol' set up by King Manasseh in the Temple. Although this idol was later removed, Ezekiel's use of the word may mean that a replica, if not the original, was put back. The word also occurs in Phoenician writings.

Some think that only the stand of the image was there, because of the reference to 'seat' in v. 3, but v. 5 refers to the image itself. Perhaps the image was taken off its stand and carried in procession, and then replaced.

This image moved God to jealousy (3). Note the way in which jealousy is ascribed to God in connection with alternative gods (Exod. **20**.5; **34**.14; Deut. **4**.24). There is nothing derogatory in it. God is jealous for our total devotion, not only for His own sake but for ours.

Consider the contrast between v. 3 and v. 4.

Ezekiel 8.7-18   Deviant Religions

Many Christians reading this chapter today find it rather remote from their experience unless they have had encounters with Satanism and witchcraft. But Celtic missionaries to Britain encountered this sort of syncretistic worship as they formed Christian communities, and many younger churches all over the world have members who are tempted to add the spirits of the old religion to their Christian religion. Ezekiel sees three forms of worship.

(*i*) *A secret society for the élite* (7–13). Christianity has always been open to all. By contrast there are pseudo-Christian and non-Christian movements that offer secrets to people who like to feel that they have something exclusive. Paul deals with such people in Col. **2**. Ezekiel sees 70 men, superior elders, worshipping animal spirits in a secret room. The room was perhaps too small to accommodate idols, so the best artists had depicted Egyptian, Mesopotamian, and Canaanite animal deities in pictures on the walls. Outstanding among the worshippers was the son of Shaphan. Shaphan had been King Josiah's right-hand man at the time of the Reformation (2 Kings **22**.3 ff.). They justified their new religion on the ground that God had deserted the land (cf. Isa. **28**.14,15; Zeph. **1**.12).

(*ii*) *A religion for women* (14,15). Nature religions commonly contain a ritual for the god of vegetation and life, who dies in the autumn and comes to life in the spring. Tammuz, Adonis,

21

Osiris, Baldur, are all variants of beautiful young gods who are mourned by devoted women when they die each year. By contrast Jehovah is the living God (Deut. **5.**26; Psa. **42.**2). Yet even He became Man in order to die once, and only once, for the sins of the world (Heb. **9.**26).

(*iii*) *Worship of the sun* (16–18). These worshippers showed their contempt for God by standing in such a way that they had their backs to the Temple while they reverenced the sun (cf. 2 Kings **23.**5,11), worshipping the creature rather than the Creator (Rom. **1.**25). The branch held to the nose may have been in imitation of the Egyptian *ankh*, a symbol of life, which is shown in carvings as held to the nose, or it may have been connected with plants sacred to Tammuz or some other god. The word 'branch' here is the same as 'slips' in Isa. **17.**10.

If I enjoy all that is mine in Christ, there is no need to look further (*Col. 2.3*).

Ezekiel 9 The Great Division

Within the city, rotten to the heart, God knows His own people. Ezekiel has already been shown that God accepts responsibility for the destruction of the city and consequent exile (ch. **5**). So now he sees, not the Babylonians, but angelic messengers of destruction. They march in past the image of jealousy and the mourners for Tammuz, and take their stand near the sun-worshippers, invisible to all except Ezekiel.

Before they start their mission of death, one of their number, in appearance like a scribe, is sent to mark the foreheads of all who truly care about the declension from God. There is a prophetic significance in the Hebrew word for the mark (4). It is the Hebrew letter T (Tau), which at that time was written as a cross. Without being superstitious we can rejoice in this anticipation of salvation through the death of Christ on the cross.

The Cross separates the living from the dead (6). One of the most awful sentences in Scripture is 'Begin at My sanctuary' (6). It is possible to be involved in religion up to the hilt, and yet to be away from God and under His judgement (Rev. **3.**1–6).

Ezekiel sees all this happen symbolically. When the reality came, there were enough faithful men, women, and children who were saved to join the nucleus of the repentant and restored nation later. Yet it was true that God did not pity the nation as it was (10), in the sense of relenting, to allow them to continue as before.

The last word of the chapter lies with the scribe (11). Whatever may be the fate of the rebels, he has found all God's true servants, and none of them is lost.

Compare this marking with Rev. 7.3, 4; 13.16; 14.9; 20.4; 22.4.

Ezekiel 10. 1-8   The Glory Prepares to Go

The glorious presence of the Lord prepares to leave the Temple. Ezekiel sees a vision of God and the cherubim that is virtually the same as that which he had seen in Babylonia. God is not limited by distance. Ezekiel now records faithfully what he heard and saw.

A voice tells the scribe, who had set the mark on God's true people, to take coals of fire from within the living creatures and the wheels and scatter them over the city, presumably as a symbol of destruction (2). One of the living creatures helps him, and draws out the fiery coals (7).

The interpretation of God's movement in vs. 3 and 4 is not certain. When Ezekiel describes his vision in ch. 1, he does not speak of the living creatures as cherubim. In this chapter he recognizes that this is what they were (20), and probably connects them with the cherubim over the mercy seat in the Holy of Holies. This is where God manifested Himself (Exod. 25.22; Num. 7.89; 2 Kings 19.15). The probability is, therefore, that in 9.3 and 10.4 the cherubim from which the glory of the Lord went up are the two golden cherubim in the Holy of Holies. The significance is that the glorious presence of God is leaving the Temple. The other cherubim, bearing the chariot firmament, come and stand ready to receive the glory of God (3). Note that in v. 1 the throne on the firmament is empty, in contrast to 1.26–28, so v. 4 can hardly mean that the Lord leaves the throne. The distinction between the two sorts of cherubim was obvious to Ezekiel, and is obvious to us when it is pointed out.

The sad thing was that Ezekiel was evidently the only person who saw the glory of God. The rest had eyes only for images, pictures, and the lesser glory of the sun.

Ezekiel also hears the roaring of the wings of the cherubim (5). The noise is like the voice of God Almighty. Perhaps the reference is metaphorically to the thunder, as in Psa. 29.3–9. (cf. 1.24; John 12.28,29).

'God is still on the throne.' Which throne?

Ezekiel 10.9-22   Reluctant Withdrawal

There is no need to make much of minor differences between this vision and that of ch. 1, e.g. the different order in which things are mentioned. The one puzzling difference is the faces in v. 14, where here Ezekiel speaks of cherub, man, lion, eagle, instead of man

23

(in front), lion (right), ox (left), eagle (back) in **1.10**. If we remember that Ezekiel is wrestling to convey the strange sequence of a vision, we may explain the difference by the position from which Ezekiel saw the creatures. In ch. **1** they were moving towards Ezekiel with the man's face in front. Now they are south of Ezekiel and move east, with presumably the man's face still in front but no longer facing Ezekiel. Thus the ox face of each of the four would be looking towards Ezekiel, and he calls this the first face, the face which had now become the standard cherub face from his viewpoint. The very obscurity, which has to be interpreted somewhat like this, is a mark of authenticity; it would have been so easy to tidy it up by substituting *ox*.

In v. 18 the glory of the presence of the Lord, which first left the Holy of Holies for the threshold of the Temple, now settles on the chariot throne. Then the Lord on the throne moves to the East Gate of the Temple court and pauses again. It almost seems as though at each stage of withdrawal the Lord waits to see if He is to be recalled. But the men who faced east worshipping the sun (**8.16**) must have looked through the vision at the gate: their eyes were so dazzled by the created ball of light that they could not see the True Light.

Note that when the Lord does finally return, He is seen coming back through the East Gate (**43.4**). This was presumably the gate by which Jesus Christ entered the Temple courts when He came from the Mount of Olives, and, being rejected, He left by the same gate (Matt. **21.12–17**). He also is the Glory of God (John **1.14**).

Note the phrases which describe the easy movement of the cherubim in immediate response to God's will. Is there a lesson here?

Ezekiel 11 No Room for God

This is the end of the Jerusalem visions. Ezekiel has had two indications of the coming destruction by violence (**9.7**) and by fire (**10.2,7**), but he has not seen them carried out. Now he is told to denounce a group of plotters, and suddenly he sees one of the leaders drop dead (**13**) The other leader, Jaazaniah, may be the brother of Jeremiah's opponent Hananiah, who is also the son of Azzur (Jer. **28.1**).

Commentaries differ widely over the interpretation of their words (**3**), and we can note three main possibilities.

(*i*) 'It is not yet wise to rebuild the houses outside Jerusalem that were destroyed in 597 B.C. We must trust to the city walls to protect us, as the cauldron keeps the flesh inside it from the flames'.

(*ii*) 'We cannot rebuild the houses, but, if we stay as we are, we

24

shall be cooked. So let us make a pact with Egypt against Babylon' (cf. Jer. 37.5–10).

(*iii*) Follow margin, 'Is not the time near . . . ?' or Greek Septuagint, 'Are not the houses recently built?' The thought then could be, 'The bones and rubbish have gone into exile; we are left as the tasty meat'.

These plotters had also been guilty of oppression and violence (6,12). Now they will suffer in their turn (7–12). The visionary (?) death of Pelatiah is a foretaste (13).

The section vs. 14–21 favours interpretation (*iii*) above. The Jews in Jerusalem despised those like Ezekiel who had already gone into exile. Now we can see the link with the vision in ch. 1. The presence of God is not tied to Jerusalem: indeed God is now leaving the Temple. Yet those who are in exile still enjoy God as their sanctuary (16), and Ezekiel's vision in ch. 1 demonstrated His presence in Babylonia: there was the same glorious God as had been in the Temple.

Now for the first time Ezekiel speaks in miniature of the future return. He develops this theme later. The return involves both repentance and renewal (17–20).

Finally, God is seen leaving the city by way of the Mount of Olives (23). It is no coincidence that some 600 years later Christ ascended from the same mountain close to Bethany which is on the south-east slopes (Luke 24.50; Acts 1.12).

Are there such things as holy places? If so, what makes them holy?

Questions for further study and discussion on Ezekiel chs. 6–11

1. How far does God here regard the nation as a whole, and how far is He concerned with a faithful nucleus?
2. What picture do these chapters give of social evils in Judah?
3. What is wrong with idolatry?
4. Draw a tentative diagram of the cherubim, the wheels, and the chariot-throne.
5. What other passages in Scripture show that God is a sanctuary for His people wherever they are (11.16)?

Ezekiel 12   No Empty Signs

This chapter falls into three sections. Although uttered in Babylon, it reveals the impending doom of Jerusalem.

(*i*) *Sign of exile* (1–16). Ezekiel packs a rucksack with bare necessities, and walks out of the house with it in broad daylight. When night is falling, he repeats the sign, only now he digs a hole in the wall of his house and crawls out like an escaping prisoner with his face covered to obscure his sight. Next day he gives the meaning. Many in Jerusalem will pack their bags for exile with whatever they can salvage. In particular King Zedekiah will creep out of the city walls by night (12; 2 Kings 25.4), but the Lord plans for him to be caught and brought to Babylon. He will, however, come as a blind man (13; 2 Kings 25.7). Others will be scattered through different countries (15). We know that many went to Egypt (Jer. 43.7).

(ii) *Sign of terror* (17–20). Ezekiel eats his meals with his hands trembling, and glancing around all the time as though he expects an enemy to spring on him. The picture is of exiles being rounded up; all possible refuges have been demolished, and at any moment their guards may decide to beat them up (Jer. 40.1).

(iii) *Scorn of prophecy* (21–28). Ezekiel and Jeremiah had clearly been speaking of the coming destruction for some months. Yet nothing had happened, and people were growing sceptical (22). Rival prophets were foretelling a speedy return to a flourishing Jerusalem (24; 13.16; Jer. 28.1–4; 29.8,9,15,21). God warns the people that the doom is certain. It will not be delayed much longer (25).

The concluding verses say much the same, but from a slightly different angle. Whereas some were saying there would be no destruction of Jerusalem, others did not deny this, but thought it would not come for centuries (27). We are reminded of modern attitudes, such as the idea that we cannot see the hand of God in history: that we can accept the piling up of national and international evils without reference to the judgement of God: that we need not think of the possibility of the Lord's return in our lifetime, since science cannot admit supernatural interventions (2 Pet. 3.4).

Look up other passages which make light of God's apparent inaction, e.g. Isa. 5.19; Zeph. 1.12; Mal. 2.17; Matt. 24. 48–51.

Ezekiel 13 Bogus Prophecy and Magic

The people were puzzled by prophets who spoke in the Name of the Lord, but who turned out to be false (1–16, cf. Jer. 23). They appeared to have the visions, voices, and ecstatic experiences of the true prophets, but their messages came from the depths of their own mind—many today would call it their Unconscious (2; Jer. 23.16). They never spoke of repentance, but guaranteed that the blessings of God were just around the corner. We are reminded of the so-called Cargo Cults in Melanesia, where the people wait passively for the predicted arrival of a Messianic figure in a great ship or plane, bringing a cargo of all the luxuries which the white man has kept for himself.

These prophets did not strengthen the moral defences of the nation (5), but painted the shoddy façades to make them look good (10, cf. Jer. 6.14). This temptation faces us today with rotten books and pictures. Many justify them, but our national resistance crumbles under the storms (11–13).

Another ancient and modern perversion is magic and superstition (17–23). Occult forces can be mobilized against other people through suggestion and, probably, directly. In Babylonia Jewish women were selling charms and spells. They were ready to do anything for even a small reward, putting a curse on the innocent, and promising a long and safe life for wrongdoers (19).

It is not easy to know the form of their spells. They certainly used armbands and veils, and it seems that these were first placed on their clients (18), and then on the witch (20,21). The order and the context suggest that the veils were worn to preserve life and probably bring luck. The armbands were destructive. Perhaps something belonging to one's enemy was taken to the witch, who folded it in a handkerchief, and tied it to the wrist of the client with some recital of spells. She then transferred it to her own arm, and projected a curse into it while she continued to wear it.

Note. RSV disguises the fact that 'souls' in vs. 18 and 20 and 'persons' in v. 19 represent the same Hebrew word *nephesh*. A consistent translation of either 'souls' or 'persons' would be better.

For other occasions of testing (11–14) note Isa. 28.16–18; Matt. 7.24–27; 1 Cor. 3.11–15.

Ezekiel 14.1-11   Deception

This is an important passage concerning finding out the will of God and doing it. It arises when some leaders of the nation come to Ezekiel to hear a message from God. Yet they are idolaters, either literally (as in Isa. 48.5 which refers to the exile, even though written before the exile), or morally and spiritually (as in Matt. 6.24). It would seem as though they wanted to hear God's will, and then decide whether they would do it: would it fit their pattern of life, or would it cause too much upheaval (cf. Jer. 42.5,6; 43.1–4)?

This is making mockery of God. So far from giving a reassuring message through the prophet, God will take the questioner at his face value. He has chosen to be on the side of God's enemies, so God will treat him as an enemy, with the hope that the suffering will bring about true repentance of heart (4–6).

Yet suppose a prophet does give a spurious answer in the Name of the Lord? God accepts responsibility for deceiving him (9). This is an important principle of God's working. If we have some great gift and are being used in the service of God, and then try to use it in our own interests, or divorce it from the requirements of Christian living, God may turn the gift against us. A theologian, who abandons revealed truth for clever ideas of his own, first deceives himself, and then, by divine rule, becomes blind to the truth. A Christian worker, who deceives himself by unwise relationships, may, by divine rule, become so blind that he brings moral chaos on himself and his family. The Hebrew mind, looking to the way in which God has ordered cause and effect in physical, moral, and spiritual spheres, might say that, if a man threw himself over a cliff, God had destroyed him; we would introduce God's 'law' of gravitation as an intermediate link in the chain.

Note some other places in Scriptures where the working of God-given laws is referred to as God's action, e.g. Isa. 6.9, 10: Matt. 13.14, 15; Exod. 4.21; 7.22; 8.15; Rom. 1.24, 25.

Ezekiel 14.12—15.8   Who will be Saved?

One of Ezekiel's central messages is *individual responsibility*. Here is one aspect of it. It is not divorced from *corporate responsibility*, and the Bible is concerned with both group and individual. In ch. **18** Ezekiel, under God, will discuss whether the individual can break the chain of evil that has come from the past. Here he makes the point that a nation cannot shelter under the goodness of a few individuals. Some thirty years previously this is what had happened with King Josiah. He had carried through a great reformation (2 Kings **22,23**), but the contemporary and subsequent words of Jeremiah show that the people did not go with him in their hearts.

Ezekiel contemplates greater characters than Josiah, three outstandingly good men, Noah, Daniel, and Job. Even their presence would not save the country in its hour of crisis, unless the people listened to them and followed their example (cf. Jer. **15**.1).

It is not easy to draw the frontier line in the O.T. between physical life and the new eternal life of God. Since so little is revealed about eternal life until after the coming of Jesus Christ, the O.T. has to speak on a physical level and we may need to transmute it on to the higher level. Not all the good men in Jerusalem survived the destruction of the city (14,16,18,20) but all were preserved in life.

The remainder of ch. **14**, in fact, speaks of survivors who are far from righteous. This, of course, does not exclude righteous survivors (9.4–6), but tells the exiles that when they find these fresh exiles flooding into Babylonia, they will see that Ezekiel has not been exaggerating the black picture he has drawn of them.

Chapter 15 is a brief parable about the wood, not this time the fruit, of the vine. God, the Divine Carpenter, has not been able to make anything out of the vine nation. Now that it has been partly charred by the fires of judgement, it is even more useless, and it must be burnt up (with v. 4, cf. John 15.6). We must take the parable, like other parables, as it is, and not look for points that it is not intended to illustrate. From another angle Isaiah drew a similar lesson from the illustration of the fruit (5.1–7).

Note on 14.14: Daniel may be the Daniel who was becoming known at the court of Nebuchadnezzar. Or his link with Noah and Job may equate him with an ancient righteous king of whom we read in Canaanite literature—a sort of King Arthur.

Consider how far we are relying on other people's righteous activity in church life.

Ezekiel 16.1-34 The Unfaithful Wife

The Bible sees human marriage as a symbol of the relationship between God and His people, just as our parental relationship symbolizes the relationship between God and ourselves (Eph.5.25–33; 3.14,15). So here, and in ch. 23, Ezekiel graphically works out the picture of Israel as the unfaithful wife, a picture found also in Hos. 1–3; Jer. 2; Isa. 1.21; 50.1.

Ezekiel begins with the city of Jerusalem, which was an old Canaanite foundation (3; Gen. 14.18). Amorites and Hittites both held Palestine during the second millennium B.C.

Note the birth customs (4) and the willingness to throw out girl babies at birth (5), a custom which lingered until well after the time of Christ.

Ezekiel passes from the city to the people of Israel who came to occupy it. It is difficult to apply a fixed stage in history for each picture, but we perhaps have the move from the wandering Abraham and his descendants (6, 7; Gen. 15), through the Sinai covenant (8; Exod. 6.6–8), to the time when David captured Jerusalem, and he and Solomon beautified it (9–14).

The phrase in v. 8 describes the symbolic act whereby the husband took his wife under his protection (Ruth 3.9). In v. 10 the Hebrew word for 'leather' is the same as is used for the covering of the Tabernacle (Exod. 25.5, where RSV has 'goatskins'). There is no need to suppose that this leather was from one sort of animal only. 'Silk' is just possible as a translation of the material in v. 13, although there are no records of its import from China until after the time of Ezekiel. The nose ring (12) was a regular ornament (Gen. 24.47; Isa. 3.21).

There are two charges of unfaithfulness and promiscuity:

(i) *With idols* (15–22). Some were crude male deities (17). Others were deities like Moloch to whom children were offered in sacrifice to be burnt in the fire (20,21). For the theme of v. 17, cf. Hos. 2.5–8. For the sacrifice of children, cf. Jer. 7.30–32; 19.4,5; 32.35.

(ii) *With foreign countries* (23–34). This also is compared to adultery in Hos. 8.9. There was always the desire to form alliances with Egypt or Assyria as a way of escape, instead of sincerely turning to God. Ezekiel contemptuously declares that Israel got nothing out of these other nations (33,34). With vs. 24,25, cf. Isa. 57.7–9.

Compare with this section, Eph. 5.25–33.

Ezekiel 16.35–63   Worse than her Sisters

The glamour fades from the spurious lovers and they become destroyers (35–41). This is how the Bible always views sin; it may be fascinating for the moment, but its wages are death (Rom. 6.23; Heb. 11.25). Note how God also accepts responsibility for the destruction (42,43). When we cycle with the wind, it is our friend; when we cycle against it, it is our enemy. Remember that the Bible often gives one aspect of God's character and dealings at a time. Here we are shown a city and nation that is thoroughly rotten and godless. In other places we are shown groups within the nation who hear and turn to God.

In v. 44 the picture changes slightly. Judah is grouped with other peoples who had low morals and low religion. She is a true daughter of Canaan, who ignored the true God and sacrificed her children (45). She is a sister of Samaria and her dependent towns ('daughters'), and of Sodom and her dependants and associates, but her standards are even lower (47,51). The sins of Sodom here include what we know of from Gen. 18.20–19.11, but go wider into the luxuries and sins of civilized prosperity (49,50; Gen. 13.10).

The section 53–55 presents a difficulty. History shows that Samaria was restored, and the Samaritans became a flourishing community. Sodom, however, is still buried. Ezekiel probably has two groups in mind. Samaria represents those who in the past were a breakaway from Judah. Sodom represents the dregs of Canaanite society, and would be those who had not had any allegiance to Jehovah (cf. Matt. 10.15; 11.23,24). Note that in each case 'her daughters' takes the picture further than the individual city mentioned.

Thus God says here that Samaria and Canaanite cities will be released one day from the dominion of Babylon and rebuilt. After the return from exile, all the land had a measure of relief, and many ultimately turned to the true God, before and after the time of Christ (Mark 7.26).

What then would happen to Judah? Would she be excluded from the restoration? This is the theme of vs. 60–63. The covenant will be renewed (cf. Jer. 31.31–34), and the people will be ashamed of their old ways. As a fact of history the Jews absorbed the nations of Palestine, and by the time of Christ there was a measure of unity in the land (61).

Consider vs. 49, 50 as applicable to nations today.

Ezekiel 17 — Allegories of Transplanting

Among other things this chapter contains a criticism of King Zedekiah. He had made a pact, binding him by oath to Babylon, but he broke it in the hope of help from Egypt. Both Jeremiah and Ezekiel accused him of disloyalty, and urged submission to Babylon again (Jer. 37.6–10; 38.17–23).

The general theme of the allegories is clear in the light of the comments in vs. 11–21.

(*i*) The Babylonian eagle takes King Jehoiachin from Judah to Babylon in 597 B.C. (3,4; 2 Kings 24.8–16; 25.27–30).

(*ii*) The Babylonian eagle makes Zedekiah king in Judah. Note the meaning of 'low spreading' given in 13,14 (5,6; 2 Kings 24.17).

(*iii*) The Egyptian eagle attracts Zedekiah and his people (7). The exact meaning of the final words of v. 7 and the following verse is far from clear in the RSV. The Egyptian eagle did not transplant anyone to Egypt at this time, although he had taken Jehoahaz in 609 B.C. (2 Kings 23.31–35). Since the margin shows that the Hebrew text has 'it was transplanted', it is preferable to retain this, as the AV and RV do, whether or not we run the two verses together. Then the reference is back to v. 5. Zedekiah had been taken up from the royal family and replanted as king by Babylon, without his needing to turn to Egypt.

(*iv*) Zedekiah and his people will be uprooted. There is a further problem of 'he' in v. 9, but it could be the king of Babylon. While the switch from Egypt to Babylon would be too violent with 'he' in v. 8, it would be less abrupt here. But v. 20 perhaps indicates that 'he' here could be God Himself.

(*v*) Ultimately God will bring His Messiah, presumably from the line of the king already in Babylon (22–24). The word 'sprig' links on to the Messianic title of 'branch' in Isa. 11.1; Jer. 23.5; 33.15; Zech. 3.8; 6.12. Three Hebrew words are used. Ezekiel's word is the feathery top of a tree; the other words describe the shoot coming from the stump of the line of David. The nations find shelter under the Messiah (23, cf. Matt. 13.31,32). The 'mountain height of Israel' is a term that looks beyond the literal Jerusalem (cf. Isa. 2.2,3; Heb. 12.22–24). What a fine ending to a gloomy chapter!

Consider the importance of keeping one's word (e.g. Psa. 15.4). Breaking the covenant with Babylon is breaking the covenant with God (19).

Ezekiel 18   The Past and the Present

There was a proverb circulating in Jerusalem (Jer. 31.29) and Babylon in which the present generation blamed their sufferings on the sins of their fathers. To a certain extent this was true, but Jeremiah and Ezekiel challenge the false conclusion that they could now do nothing about it. The second commandment (Exod. 20.5,6) had spoken of the cumulative disaster that mounts up when generation after generation refuses to repent. This is also the teaching of Jesus Christ (Matt. 23.35,36). Ezekiel asserts that each generation is responsible for breaking the evil tradition or for maintaining the good one. We must learn from our parents by way of example and warning.

The sins in vs. 5–8 are both religious and moral, and all are found in the Law, after the references to special forms of idol worship in v. 6 (cf. 6.1–7), e.g. (in order) Exod. 20.14; Lev. 18.19; Exod. 22.26–27; Exod. 20.15; Deut. 15.7–11; Exod. 22.25; Exod. 23.6–9.

Note that the Bible does not condemn all lending of money at interest as wrong in itself, e.g. Deut. 23.20; Luke 19.23. But it envisages interest-free loans to God's people who are in real need.

Note the sequences in this chapter; good father—bad son—good son. Commentators differ over the extent of the term 'die' in this chapter. Sheer fact, of which Ezekiel was as fully aware as we are, makes it impossible to limit it to physical death, but physical death in Scripture is linked with eternal death. It would, however, be wrong to emphasize 'soul' in v. 4 as though it were intended as a contrast to 'body'. The latter word does not occur here, and the Hebrew *nephesh* often means no more than 'person' (e.g. Exod. 1.5).

Although v. 24 raises difficulties in the N.T. context of the final perseverance of the saints, such warnings must stand in Scripture.

No person—believer or unbeliever—ever has the right to say, 'Because I was righteous once, it does not matter whether I am plunging into sin now.'

The chapter ends (25–32) with an appeal to turn to God in repentance from their twisted ideas about Him. Thus they will 'get' a new heart, which is, of course, the gift of God (**11.**19; **36.**26).

Consider the importance of vs. 23 and 32.

Ezekiel 19 Lion Hunt

The RSV carefully sets this chapter out as poetry, printing the lines according to the balance of the rhythm. This is known as the *qīnāh* or 'lamentation metre', which we have already noticed in the *Book of Lamentations*. It is worth reading aloud.

The lament is for three kings of Judah. There is no doubt about the first being Jehoahaz who was taken prisoner to Egypt in 609 B.C. (3,4; 2 Kings **23.**31–33). Commentators usually identify the second with Jehoiachin, who was taken to Babylon in 597 B.C. (5–9), and the third with Zedekiah, who was king at the destruction of Jerusalem in 586 B.C. (10–14). The puzzling thing is the omission of Jehoiakim, who succeeded Jehoahaz and reigned 609–598 B.C. Possible explanations are:

(*i*) Jehoahaz and Jehoiachin are selected because they both shared the fate of exile. Since they reigned for no more than about three months each, the language of vs. 3,4,6,7 must represent their potentialities as their mother saw them.

(*ii*) The second is Jehoiakim, who was taken to Babylon for a short period (2 Chron. **36.**6; Dan. **1.**2), although he actually died during the siege of Jerusalem (2 Kings **24.**1–6). The third king is then Jehoiachin (10–12), and the contemporary king Zedekiah is only part of the ruin, without the strength a ruler needs (13,14).

Notes: The symbol of the lioness as the mother of the kings of Judah links up with Gen. **49.**9, cf. Rev. **5.**5 of Christ.

In vs. 4 and 9 the hooks are appropriate to wild beasts, but they were also used for prisoners. The Assyrian king, Ashurbanipal, kept a king on exhibition in a cage at Nineveh (9).

In v. 14 note that the destructive fire comes from the stem of the vine itself. Thus Jerusalem and the royal house are the cause of their own destruction. Note how Ezekiel follows through the picture of this verse to a glorious end in **21.**25–27.

The closing note by the final compiler of the book probably indicates that this lamentation had passed into regular use as a dirge.

Consider when we should lament for leaders.

Questions for further study and discussion on Ezekiel chs. 12—19

1. Sir Robert Anderson wrote a book called 'The Silence of God'. Consider this as a title for these chapters.
2. How far are magic and superstition attempts to have the supernatural without the moral and spiritual claims of God?
3. How does the N.T. keep the balance between individual and corporate responsibility?
4. Why is the breaking of a promise or covenant regarded as such a serious crime in the Bible, and why is it so lightly regarded today?
5. How far does a nation share responsibility when its leaders are bad?

Ezekiel 20.1-22 Verdict of History

It is easy to come, as the elders did, to get a message from God's minister. It is less easy to listen to a diagnosis of blind rebellion—blind because we have not seen that we are perpetuating the self-centredness of our forefathers. Thus Ezekiel expounds history in the light of God's honour and the nation's disregard of Him. Note the repetition here and elsewhere in *Ezekiel* of 'for the sake of My name'. This does not mean that God refuses to act out of love for people, but is concerned only with His own reputation. God's people are intended to be the reflection of God's own character (Exod. **19**.6; Lev. **11**.44,45). Their poor behaviour gives the outsider a poor view of God's character.

In this chapter God reviews the different periods of Israel's history.

Egypt (5–9). This is the only place where God says that He told Israel to avoid idolatry in Egypt. The probability is that the strong action of Jacob in Gen. **35**.1–4, in making all his household put away pagan gods, was the word of God for his descendants in Egypt. The fact that they turned so easily to fresh idols like the golden calf, indicates that many, as Ezekiel says, must have been attracted also by Egyptian religious practices.

The Wilderness (10–22). The first major thing that God did was to give His people rules for living (11), i.e. the Law, and an inner and outward mark of devotion to Himself, i.e. the weekly Sabbath (12). During the next few readings note Ezekiel's emphasis on the Sabbath. His contemporary, Jeremiah, also emphasized its observance as a mark of spiritual vitality (Jer. **17**.21–27). There are two examples of profaning the Sabbath during this time (Exod. **16**.27; Num. **15**.32), but the accusation here must include the general

34

attitude towards the worship of God (note v. 16). Underground hankering after idols made Sabbath worship a pure formality (cf. Isa. 1.13). The significance of v. 22 is that, if God had not ultimately brought the people into the promised land, the Egyptians and others would have thought He was unable to do so (Exod. 32.12).

Psalm 106 may profitably be read alongside of this chapter.

Ezekiel 20.23-49   Man's Choice—and God's

This section (23-31) continues the earlier history of rebellion. In the wilderness the people were warned of the consequences of diobedience and idolatry when they came into the land (23, Lev. 26; Deut. 28). Yet they disobeyed, and consequently God gave them up to the degradation of Canaanite worship (26, 27), which accompanied the glamour of the high place ceremonies (28,29). If we link the thoughts of vs. 25 and 26 with Rom. 1.24-32, we can see that there is no contradiction between this passage and·Jer. 7.31, which says that God did not command these things. God abandoned them to the customs and consequences of the religion they had chosen. *Bamah* is the regular word for 'high place', and v. 29 is a punning connection with *mah* ('what') and *bo* ('go'). Whatever its original derivation, the Hebrews took it from the Canaanites. God asks them to consider what is this place of worship that they unthinkingly patronize.

Next (32-39) God speaks of the sifting out of the idolaters. He will not allow them to continue their syncretistic religion (32), but will deal with them in exile. The wilderness (35,36) is clearly not literal, but a wilderness of experience. Before the Shepherd admits the flock to His land, He will separate the sheep from the goats (37,38).

The restored community will be a holy and devoted group (40-44). The tragedy was that those who returned with such enthusiasm, as we read in *Ezra* and *Nehemiah*, gradually slipped back again, though not into the crudities of high place worship and human sacrifice. The history between the Old and New Testaments is often a sad one, but with a strong nucleus of firm believers.

In vs. 45-49 there is a fresh type of prophecy, which perhaps is to be linked with the next chapter. One might have supposed that, if Nebuchadnezzar were invading from the north, the south would escape. But this is not to be, and the picture of the blazing trees moves to the blaze which will burn the whole nation. Thus

35

Ezekiel speaks an allegory for those who have ears to hear (cf. Isa. 2.13,14).

Compare this chapter with Jer. 3.6 and 7.30–34.

Ezekiel 21   The Sword of the Lord

The jerkiness of vs. 1–17 is probably due to something that Ezekiel is doing. Since he and other prophets often reinforced their messages with dramatic signs, he has perhaps drawn a sword and is whirling it round, making it flash in the sun, and shouting his words in disjointed sentences. Yet these sentences are linked by a vital theme: The Lord had used a stick of wood to chastise His people, but they had treated it as of no account (10,13). Now He has drawn the cutting sword of invasion, siege and capture, and in such an event both good and bad die or are taken into exile (4). The sword that Ezekiel displays is not just a threat, but continues where the rod leaves off (13), i.e. the day of warning is over. The N.T. treats the Second Coming in similar terms. One may ignore the warnings of history, but the final Day of the Lord cannot be ignored (cf. v. 7 with Luke 21.26).

In vs. 18–23 Babylon is invading. Nebuchadnezzar tosses up to see whether to besiege Jerusalem or Rabbah. Where we might toss a coin, Nebuchadnezzar's diviners judged by the fall of arrows, shaken and thrown down; by some consultation of images; and by signs in the liver of a sacrifice (21). Jerusalem is chosen. All the same, the people of Jerusalem do not believe that the decision will be effective (23). The remainder of v. 23 is difficult, but perhaps means that Zedekiah is guilty of breaking his oath of allegiance to Nebuchadnezzar (2 Kings 24.20).

This, however, does not exhaust the meaning, since the following verses show that both people and king are rotten at heart. Yet v. 27 is one of the great Messianic promises of the O.T., although it is often overlooked. It is similar to the promise of Gen. 49.10, (RSV). After the exile there were no more kings of David's line. Zerubbabel, who was leader soon after the return, was of David's line, but was never king.

Finally God speaks to Ammon (28–32), who had escaped the Babylonian attack, and who in fact turned against Judah and exploited her defeat (25.3). Ammon's turn will come for the sword, and her name will be forgotten (32).

'Whose right it is' (27). 'The highest place that heaven affords is His, is His, by right.' Why 'by right'? (See Phil. 2.5–11; Rev. 5.9–14.)

36

It is only too easy to read these accusations simply as descriptions of the state of Jerusalem immediately before the exile. The fact is that most great nations have taken the same road. The words could have been written of Assyria, Babylon, Greece, and Rome, in their days of decadent domination. We do well to watch the contemporary situation. While there is considerable desire to help the underprivileged and the sufferer today, governments and power blocks continue to create fresh areas of misery, sometimes violently. The claims of God give way to the worship of man's inventions. Family life is disrupted, and abnormal sexual behaviour is advertised by films and books. Even our responsibility towards our neighbour goes by the board if through its abuse or abandonment we can make a little extra for ourselves. All these wrongs are found in vs. 1–12.

Israel and Judah were more fortunate than other nations which disintegrated when their morality exploded (Mal. 3.6). God took His people into exile, but used the exile to clean and renew them (13–16), even though, at first, their life gave the outsider a poor impression of God (16).

Meanwhile the siege approaches, and the country people crowd into Jerusalem for protection (19). They will be like metal and dross in a cauldron, with the fire blazing underneath. The point of the comparison here is not that the dross rises to the surface so that it can be skimmed off, but that the solid metal is melted into a fluid mass. All are subjected to judgement. The picture of refining is used also in Psa. 12.6; Prov. 17.3; Isa. 1.25; 48.10; Jer. 6.28–30; Mal. 3.2,3; 1 Pet. 1.7. Although the RSV makes v. 18 match v. 20 (see margin), the order of the Hebrew text makes reasonable sense, i.e. 'all of them are brass . . . in the midst of the furnace; they are the dross of silver' (RV).

The final charge is against the men in power who misused their position (25,27. What is power today?), religious leaders who abandoned what God had revealed (26), and prophetic preachers, who spoke easy platitudes (28). Small wonder that the ordinary masses had slipped morally (29). If only there had been God's men to speak and to act! (30, cf. Isa. 59.16; Jer. 5.1).

Consider v. 14. Habits of wrong living (13) sap our courage and strength when the hour of trial comes

Ezekiel 23.1-21   Broken Relationship

For the second time (ch. 16) Ezekiel takes up the picture of Judah as the unfaithful wife, but now he gives prominence to unfaithful Israel also, as does Jeremiah in 3.6–10.

'Oholah' means either 'tent' or 'possessing tents'. The reference could be to the original wilderness state before the people were settled in towns (cf. Jer. 2.2), or, if the picture of the tent is that of a dwelling, God dwelt among the Northern Kingdom and had His true followers there (e.g. 1 Kings 19.18). The word used of the Tabernacle is basically the same. 'Oholibah' means 'my tent is in her', probably with reference to God's special dwelling in the Temple in Jerusalem.

The chapter does not make pleasant reading. Perhaps our danger has been in looking at the sins of God's people too academically. We disapprove of them at an intellectual level. But the crude descriptions here stir our deepest emotions. Persistent sin is not just something for which God gives us a bad mark. It is a horror of broken relationship that, if we could see it with God's eyes, would shake us as much as does the story of these two sluts.

The danger of commenting like this is that those readers who are too introspective may be driven into themselves beyond what is right. Notice, therefore, how the two wives are pictured in self-centred indulgence, which they welcome and do not resist. They are not to be compared to those Christians who know both victory and defeat with sins that attack them, and who keep looking to the Lord.

We are more likely to be overlooking sins of unfaithfulness, while we build up patterns of behaviour which fit the standards of the world rather than the way of God. Mammon comes in various disguises (Matt. 6.24), as well as in the disguise of Assyria and Babylon, and our energies may go into self-advancement (for which Assyria and Babylon offered enticing prospects) rather than into devotion to God.

For examples of appeals to foreign nations, see such passages as 2 Kings 16.7; Isa. 7.17–25; Hos. 7.11. There is no direct reference elsewhere to overtures to Babylon (16, also v. 40), but foreign alliances produced foreign standards of life and religion (e.g. 2 Kings 16.10 f.; Isa. 2.6; Jer. 7.18).

Rev. 17.1, 2; 18.1–10 are somewhat of a parallel to this chapter.

Ezekiel 23.22-49 The End of it All

The orgies end in death. The lovers, with no ties of marriage, terminate the affair when they wish. All the rag, tag, and bobtail join in the humiliation of Oholibah. Pekod (23) is a tribe east of the Tigris (Jer. 50.21), and Shoa and Koa have been identified with other tribes in the same area. Even the Assyrians, conquered and absorbed by the Babylonians (Chaldeans), are in the Babylonian attack on Jerusalem. Cruelties like those described in v. 25 were actually practised, and physical brutalities on prisoners of war and political detainees are unfortunately not unknown today.

There is a profound psychological truth in vs. 28, 29 (cf. 17). Sex without love only too often ends in frustration and hatred (2 Sam. 13.15). Quite apart from sex without marriage, a marriage that is grounded simply on physical attraction is likely to collapse, because there is no union of mind and spirit.

In vs. 32–34 Ezekiel uses a new metaphor, that of a cup of wine which makes the drinker dead drunk. To us this is a strange picture of God's judgement, but it occurs elsewhere in Scripture, e.g. Psa. 75.8; Jer. 25.15 f.; Lam. 4.21; Rev. 14.10; 16.19. The symbolism is that of the drunkard who collapses helplessly, and who is then a victim for his enemies as well as an ultimate misery to himself. The contents of God's cup have a similar effect. We have seemed to ourselves to be so strong that we could defy God's standards and even God Himself; suddenly in the crisis we are helpless. Today our fresh knowledge of the plight of the alcoholic can vary Ezekiel's illustration. The alcoholic is not, of course, more wicked than others, but he cannot achieve contented sobriety so long as he goes his own way and believes that next time the crisis comes he will be strong enough to conquer. Only when he comes to the end of himself and casts himself upon God can he stop destroying himself.

The closing verses (36–49) are a summary of all that has gone before.

The formation of habit-responses is part of our God-given personality. It is vital to see that our habits are constructive and not destructive (Phil. 3.19; 4.11–13).

Ezekiel 24.1-14 The Rusty Pot

Like most preachers Ezekiel uses an illustration more than once, varying the application according to the point of his message. He has used the picture of the cauldron in 11.3–12. Now he takes it up again. Jerusalem is the cooking pot, and its people are the meat that is to be cooked. But the pot is rusty and filthy as well. When the meat is cooked up and emptied out, the pot is set on the fire again and heated until it melts, thus destroying itself with the rust and filth. Thus God declares that Jerusalem cannot be saved; it can only be destroyed.

The chapter is dated in the ninth year of Jehoiachin's captivity, which was also Ezekiel's captivity. This makes the date January, 588 B.C. Although Ezekiel is in Babylon, he is prophetically told by God that on this very day Nebuchadnezzar has begun the siege

39

of Jerusalem. The date agrees with 2 Kings 25.1. As an additional witness Ezekiel writes down the date, so that it can be checked later (2).

It is possible that the Hebrew of v. 6 (see margin) implies that at Jehoiachin's captivity captives were selected by lot. Now all will be taken indiscriminately.

The blood in v. 7 is that of murder, wrongful conviction, and human sacrifice. Blood unjustly shed cries for vengeance (Gen. 4.10; Job 16.18). The people who committed the crimes did not even trouble to conceal them (7). So God takes them at their word, and does not cover up their sins in forgiveness (8). Yet God had been willing to forgive them provided that they would let Him make them clean (12,13). The Bible looks at cleansing from both the divine and the human point of view. God Himself makes us clean (e.g. 36.25; 1 John 1.7) and yet we must make ourselves clean (e.g. Isa. 1.16; 2 Cor. 7.1). There is no practical contradiction here. We may start by saying 'No: I will go my own way'. We may then repent and begin to make the effort to reform. Then we see our own inability and call to God to do what we cannot do.

Compare what is said here about blood and cleansing with Heb. 12.24, 25.

Ezekiel 24.15-27   Deep Sorrow

It is significant that the squalor of free love in ch. 23, with the further allusions in 24.13, should be followed by the picture of the close of a happy marriage. A happy marriage is one of God's greatest gifts to mankind, as Ezekiel had found. In many respects Ezekiel was a hard man, if we are to judge by the content of his sermons, but he had to steel himself to resist the rot in the nation. Now in this sidelight we see him as a man devoted to his wife, 'the delight of his eyes'. Suddenly he loses her, and he is forbidden to mourn openly for her. We need not press v. 16 to mean that God acted in an arbitrary way, but the phrase reminds us that God's hand is to be seen even in what we call the normal processes of life. We do not know whether Ezekiel's wife was already ill.

At this moment of acute distress, God uses the tragedy as yet another prophetic sign. The meaning of this sign is not obvious to us at first sight, but the exiles in Babylon, to whom Ezekiel is speaking, must face the loss of the Temple and city, which are dear to them. When the appalling news reached them, they would be shocked into genuine mourning, far beyond what might be expressed by the traditional signs (21-24).

Ezekiel is further told that one day the news will come through a refugee. God will warn him of this previously, and he will be dumb with horror, just as he was dumb at his wife's death (17). But when the refugee arrives, he will be ready to talk freely with him (25–27, cf. 33.21,22).

For the signs of mourning mentioned here (17,22) see 2 Sam. 15.30; Isa. 20.2; Jer. 16.7; Hos. 9.4; Mic. 3.7.

It is worth noticing how marriage was used as a prophetic sign with two other prophets. Jeremiah was forbidden to marry because so many children would die in the coming siege (16.2–4). Hosea learnt from the unfaithfulness of his wife how God felt about the unfaithfulness of His people (Hos. 1–3).

God does not forbid deep emotion provided that it is real (17; Matt. 5.4; Acts 20.37, 38).

Questions for further study and discussion on Ezekiel chs. 20—24

1. In what way do these chapters show that God is the God of history?
2. Check the nations and places mentioned here, using a good map. Which were the closest neighbours of Israel and Judah?
3. Why do we assume that God is not limited by time? What indications are there in these chapters that Ezekiel was given supernatural knowledge of present and future events?
4. Does the strong language of ch. 22 justify the production of pornographic literature today?
5. In the light of 24.17, how far should a Christian normally observe the social customs of the country in which he is living at the moment?

Ezekiel 25 Ancient and Modern

As we begin this new section of the Book, we may perhaps wonder why God takes up space with nations that have long since vanished. It is significant that they have vanished. Everyone has heard of Jerusalem: few could place Rabbah, the capital of Ammon (5), or the important cities of Moab to the north-east and east of the Dead Sea (9), or Teman and Dedan in the north and south of Edom (13). Although the Philistines (15) gave their name to Palestine, they also vanished as a nation. We can speak of ourselves as members of Jerusalem and of Israel (Gal. 4.26; 6.16; Rev. 21.10,12,14), but not of Rabbah and Ammon. The gods of these nations are now no more than mythological curiosities. The God of Israel is the God of our Lord Jesus Christ, and is our God today.

Secondly, we must remember that these nations and their

threats were as real to Israel and Judah as are the great nations of our day to us. So long as nation competes with nation, these chapters are topical. The same old methods of international competition are still present, and the same old attitudes of groups of people; surely they still come under the judgement of God.

Ammon evidently took advantage of Babylon's victory and grabbed whatever land and property that they could. This is implied in v. 3 and is confirmed by Jer. **49**.1. Here is the temporarily strong nation taking advantage of the weaker neighbour. There were, of course, Jews who eluded the Babylonians and remained in the land, as members of the Northern Kingdom did after the Assyrian invasion.

Moab probably also took the opportunity of gaining extra territory, but Ezekiel singles out her sceptical attitude, which denied that there was any special relationship between Israel and the true God (8). Moab and Ammon were, in fact, soon overrun by invading Nabateans.

Edom was terribly treacherous at the fall of Jerusalem (Psa. **137**.7; Obad. 10–14). Edom also was overrun, and, eventually, in 109 B.C. it was finally subjugated by the Jewish leader, John Hyrcanus (14).

The Philistines are denounced as always looking for an occasion for war (15). The name Cherethites is probably connected with Crete, which is one of the places from which the Philistines came (Zeph. **2**.5). David had a group of Cherethite mercenaries as well as others from Gath (2 Sam. **15**.18).

Groups and nations, as well as individuals, have their own character.

Ezekiel 26   Sea Traders

It is surprising to find three whole chapters devoted to Tyre, since there is hardly any mention of her, and her fellow-city of Sidon, in the history of Israel. As these chapters indicate, the Phoenicians, who lived in the coastal strip which contained these two cities, were more concerned with sea trading than with extending their territory. At the same time they were ready to move in when the Jews and Israelites moved out (2).

Earlier Tyre had treacherously broken a pact (Amos **1**.9), and she is selected as an example of proud self-sufficiency by Isaiah (Isa. **23**) as well as by Ezekiel. One way of reading these chapters is after the pattern of Rev. **18**, where indeed some of the phraseology there applied to Babylon is applied to Tyre in *Ezekiel*, as the RSV margin here shows. Babylon and Tyre represent the attitude of civilization without the standards of God, the attitude which has come to be characterized as 'I'm all right, Jack', i.e. 'Never mind about others, so long as I have what I want—not just what I need'. This attitude rouses others to want what we have, and Babylon and Tyre become the target of other nations.

Ezekiel is given this message shortly after the fall of Jerusalem. Nebuchadnezzar now turned his attention to Tyre, which held out on its island for thirteen years. It is now known from inscriptions that Nebuchadnezzar eventually forced its submission and put a puppet king on the throne. Ezek. **29.**18 records that he did not obtain enough spoil from the city to pay for all the efforts he had made.

In fact, he did not destroy Tyre, but Alexander the Great exactly fulfilled vs. 8–14 in 332 B.C. Certain prophecies are conditional, as God says in Jer. **18.**7–11, and as Jonah found when he said by the word of God that Nineveh would be destroyed within forty days. Nineveh humbled itself and was spared for the time being, though ultimately it reached a peak of wickedness and was destroyed. Perhaps Tyre was humbled in the same way, and its doom was averted until later.

What will people connect with us when we go (17)?

*Ezekiel 27.1-24   An Affluent Society

Whereas a commentary on ch. **26** can be in general terms, this section must obviously be largely notes on the peoples and countries with whom Tyre has been trading, so far as these can be identified. We follow the RSV which sometimes renders the names differently from the AV and RV.

In vs. 3–9 Tyre is pictured as a great ship made from the finest materials. This section is in verse, as the RSV indicates, but there is no reason to regard the prose that follows (10–25) as by a different author. Like Isa. **3.**18–23 it is very much of a catalogue, which is hard to put into verse.

Wood for the ship comes from the north of Palestine (5,6). Senir (5) is the Canaanite name for Hermon (Deut. **3.**9; other references can be found under Senir and Shenir in an AV concordance). Elishah (7) is thought by some to be Enkomi on the east coast of Cyprus (also Gen. **10.**4). Sidon, the island city of Arvad, Zemer, and Gebal (known by the Greeks as Biblos), are all Phoenician coastal cities (8,9).

To defend herself Tyre had mercenaries from Persia, Lydia (Lud); and Put (10). The last named is likely to be Libya, but may be the Egyptian Punt on the African coast. Other troops come from Arvad (already mentioned), and Helech, which is probably Cilicia, and from the unidentified Gamad (11).

43

The ships of Tyre traded all over the known world. Tarshish is Tartessus in Spain (12). Javan is the name for the Greek Ionians, and Tubal and Meshech are probably peoples to the south of the Black Sea (see also **38**.2,3). Inscriptions refer to Tegarama (14) as between Carchemish and Haran on an important trade route through Armenia. Rhodes, Edom, Judah and Damascus (15–18) are well known. Helbon (18) is north-east of Damascus, while Uzal (19) is likely to be Izalla in north-east Syria, which is mentioned as supplying Nebuchadnezzar with wine.

Then the description moves to Arabia, where are the peoples mentioned in 20–22. Finally, Mesopotamian peoples and towns are listed (23). Of these, Eden is the Assyrian province of Bit-Adini between Haran and the Euphrates (cf. 2 Kings **19**.12), but Canneh and Chilmad are unidentified.

*Tyre was an affluent society—for some (13, cf. Rev. **18**.12, 13). So Luke **12**.15 is relevant.*

*Ezekiel 27.25-36   All are Involved

We began the chapter with the finest ship in the world. This was Tyre. Then came the catalogue of her greatness. Now we return to the first picture, but what a difference! The ship is shattered by the storm, and is lost with all her crew, and all her rich cargo. The poem slips easily into its application. The world is astounded at the ruin of the great trading power from whom they gained all the necessities and luxuries of life.

The collapse of a great power inevitably brings fear to others (35), for no one knows whose turn it will be next. If Nebuchadnezzar spares others now, there will soon be some other conqueror.

In v. 36 the merchants *hiss* at the fallen city. The word occurs in other passages also in connection with destruction, and is coupled with 'astonishment' (1 Kings **9**.8), 'curse' (Jer. **25**.18), 'reproach' (Jer. **29**.18), 'horror' (Jer. **51**.37), 'clapping hands, wagging the head, and gnashing teeth' (Lam. **2**.15,16). In spite of this we do not know its exact significance. It could be an expression of disapproval and rejection, as when an audience hisses bad performers. It could be the equivalent of spitting to avert the evil eye, or curse. Or it could be a whistle of amazement at what has happened, as one might say 'Phew!'

Whatever the significance the reactions of those who are not sharing Tyre's doom remind us of how we are nationally bound together. One group cannot perish or rise to power without affecting all.

'It can't happen to us.'

44

Ezekiel 28.1-10 Pride Before a Fall

This is a remarkable chapter which has been treated differently by various commentators. The main problem comes in the next portion, where one has to decide whether or not there is a description of Satan. For today's reading we can all agree that Ezekiel is describing Ithobaal II, the king of Tyre. He is here given the title of 'prince' or 'ruler' (2), which does not exclude kingship, but is commonly used of others than kings. The use of the lesser word is a suitable introduction to a chapter on pride.

The theme of the humbling of the proud has formed the subject of many stories and plays, and our own generation has seen it happen more than once. God has no room for the proud (Psa. 119.21; Luke 1.51), because pride is a denial of man's place as the servant of God, and the essence of the fall was a desire to become self-controlled, fixing one's own standards of good and evil, instead of being God-centred.

Here God strips off the disguise. The king of Tyre regards himself as the Lord of the world. He has the deep knowledge to manipulate people and markets for his own ends (4,5).

The reference to Daniel is interesting (3). There is no reason why this should not be to the Daniel at the court of Nebuchadnezzar, though he must have been still quite a young man and not very well known. Otherwise the reference is to the great and righteous Daniel of Canaanite literature which would be appropriate in addressing a Canaanite king (see note at end of ch. 14).

When the great ship of Tyre sinks, the king will perish. A ruler tends to act as though he will live for ever, like an immortal god, but each has to prove by death that he is no more than mortal (9). Before we condemn the king of Tyre, we may remember that sin in Eden was the desire to be as God (Gen. 3.5), and this desire still haunts us all. In some department of life I am almost certainly saying 'I am a god'.

By way of contrast, Phil. 2.5–11 is an excellent commentary on this. Our Lord Jesus Christ came down from the glory of Godhead, and chose to die for us as man.

Ezekiel 28.11-26 Fallen Rebel

In v. 12 the king is addressed by the regular title for king, and many Christian commentators have interpreted what follows of Satan, as king behind the rulers of this world. A similar interpretation is given to Isa. 14. Others believe that the king is here addressed as the primeval man in terms of a Phoenician version of the Eden story.

These notes will assume that the king is addressed in terms of his master, Satan. The character of Satan, here described, comes out in him. Thus this chapter and Isa. 14 throw light on the fall of Satan, and indicate that he was a created being who fell through pride.

The link with the Eden story is given near the beginning (13) to call attention to the identification with the tempter who was there; but the description of his magnificent glory belongs to his original creation and his place on the mountain of God, i.e. heaven. This description is too extravagant for Adam, though, on the interpretation it might be true of some Canaanite primeval man.

The Hebrew of v. 14 is difficult. The RV addresses him as 'Thou wast the anointed cherub that covereth'. The cherubim in the holy of holies covered the mercy seat and the ark (Exod. 25.20; 1 Kings 8.7), and symbolically guarded the approaches to God. Hence, Satan may have been once the chief guardian of the throne of God. The RSV emendation could mean that Satan had a cherub as his escort.

Neither Satan nor man was created evil (15), but both had free will, and were more than puppets or animals controlled by instinct. Both chose to be as god (Isa. 14.13,14), but the special thing that moved Satan was a desire to have yet more splendour (17). The reference to trade in v. 16 shows that there is a blend of the king of Tyre and his master. The king traded for his own power. Satan sold his glory for violent rebellion, and was cast out from the mountain of God. Again the RSV has emended the reference to the guardian cherub in v. 16, while the RV retains, 'I have destroyed thee, O covering cherub, from the midst of the stones of fire.' With the RSV, the same cherub who barred the way to Eden (Gen. 3.24) may have driven Satan from heaven.

In vs. 17–19 the earthly king comes to the fore again, but, like Satan's, his doom is inevitable. V. 18 shows that he has been concerned with fostering evil, materialistic values, and false religion, all of which carry the fire of their own destruction within them.

The remainder of the chapter concerns Tyre's neighbour, Sidon, who will not escape (20–23), and gives a brief promise of Israel's restoration (24–26). Note the allusion in v. 24 to Num. 33.55; Josh. 23.13. In ch. 34 onwards we shall be reading much more of Israel's restoration to blessing.

Satan is a rebel, not an eternal god of absolute evil. What follows from this?

Ezekiel 29.1-16   King Crocodile

The next four chapters concern Egypt. The date of this section

(1) is 587 B.C., shortly before the fall of Jerusalem. The Pharaoh addressed is Hophra, also called Apries, who had recently come to the throne. Each Pharaoh was regarded as divine, and presumably some made more of this than others. Hophra boasts that he is the maker and lord of the Nile. This is a claim that one finds in Egyptian writings, e.g. 'The Nile is at his service, and he opens its cavern to give life to Egypt.'

God addresses him as the great crocodile lying in the Nile. The word translated 'dragon' (3) denotes any monster, and the context here obviously means the crocodile. So far from owning the river, he is dragged from it and flung out on the land (4,5, cf. 32.4,5). This may have been fulfilled literally, since Hophra was deposed by a rival (cf. Jer. 44.30), and his body may well have been flung out in contempt (cf. Jer. 22.18,19).

In addition to his sin of pride, Pharaoh is charged with being a broken reed (6, cf. Isa. 36.6). The reference is to Hophra's campaign into Palestine, which temporarily caused the Babylonians to retire from the siege of Jerusalem (Jer. 37.5). But Hophra was not strong enough to carry the campaign through. He promised Judah more than he could perform, and once again his pride was humbled.

The reference to the desolation of Egypt (9–12) is probably symbolical of the subjugation of the country. From this time onwards it lost political power, after the defeat of Hophra's successor, Amasis, by Nebuchadnezzar. We do not know whether the land itself suffered disasters and famine from Migdol in the north to Syene (Assouan) in the south (10), but the symbolism could be used as the symbolism of the crocodile is used earlier. The forty years could be the symbolic equivalent of Israel's forty years of discipline in the wilderness.

The restoration of Egypt came under Greek rule, and Alexandria especially became an important centre of Judaism and Christianity, thus probably fulfilling Isa. 19.19–25. Present-day Israel would certainly appreciate v. 16.

> '*I am the master of my fate,*
> *I am the captain of my soul.*'
> *True or false? (See Josh. 24.15; Luke 12.16–21.)*

Ezekiel 29.17—30.19   Pattern of the Last Day

We noted in ch. 26 that Nebuchadnezzar eventually forced Tyre to submit, but he was unable to plunder it as he had hoped. It was easy for Tyre to remove its treasures by sea before finally submitting. Probably v. 18 refers to the Babylonian troops who were forced to carry great stones to try to build a causeway from the mainland to the island city, as Alexander the Great did later.

A Babylonian inscription says that in 568 B.C. Nebuchadnezzar fought against the army of Amasis, who had succeeded Hophra on the throne of Egypt. Josephus also records that he invaded Egypt (cf. Jer. 43.8–13). Doubtless he obtained sufficient plunder and tribute to compensate for what he had hoped to obtain from Tyre (19).

The horn of v. 21 may be the Messiah (Psa. 132.17), although it might here be simply a symbol of strength (Jer. 48.25). The following sentence could be an indication that in subsequent prophecies Ezekiel would be inspired to say more about this horn, as indeed he was in chs. 36 and 37.

In ch. 30 we have the setting of the doom of Egypt against the ultimate picture of the Day of the Lord (cf. Joel 1.15, of the locust invasion, and Isa. 13.6,9, of Babylon). The fact is that from time to time a nation reaches a climax of oppression and moral decay from which God humbles and often destroys it. The final Day is yet to come when God will put down all sin wherever it is found. Thus previous Days of the Lord become patterns of the final Day.

In 30.1–9 Egypt and all her helpers are beaten, including Ethiopia, Put (Punt on the west coast of the Red Sea), and Lydian mercenaries.

For Nebuchadnezzar's invasion (10,11), see yesterday's notes. Finally, there is a general picture of doom (12–19) falling on the many gods and goddesses of Egypt (13) and on the self-confident cities. Of the cities mentioned here, Zoan, Pelusium, Pibeseth, and Tehaphnehes (Tahpanhes), are in the Nile delta. Memphis and On (Heliopolis) are just south of the delta. Pathros is the general name for the southern part of Egypt (Upper Egypt), and Thebes is one of its cities.

What are the things mentioned here that will come under judgement on the Day of the Lord?

Ezekiel 30.20—31.18   The Withered Tree

The first prophecy here is dated about three months before the fall of Jerusalem. We have no independent evidence of what happened when Nebuchadnezzar invaded Egypt, though Josephus records that he took back a number of Jews as captives. He would undoubtedly have taken many leading Egyptians also (23,26), as was his custom when he conquered a country.

Chapter 31 is dated approximately one month before the fall of

Jerusalem (1). Now Ezekiel uses a picture of Egypt similar to that which he had used of Judah in ch. **17**. Egypt is the towering cedar, with its roots going down to the underground streams. It shelters bird and beast, and is the envy even of the trees of the garden of Eden. This is the picture that Egypt presents to itself and the world.

But in v. 10 we detect once more the Satanic impulse to pride (**28**.17), and so Egypt in her turn has to be brought low. We have already seen in ch. **29** that history records the gradual deterioration of Egypt. Although Nebuchadnezzar did not occupy it, in 525 B.C. Cambyses, king of Persia, became king of Egypt also. Two centuries later it passed into the control of Greece, and in 30 B.C. it became part of the Roman empire.

The end of Egypt is also pictured as a descent to Sheol, the place of the dead (15–18, cf. Isa. **14**.15–20). Its supply of living waters is cut off (15) and, consequently, the lesser trees that are associated with it die also. Their miserable consolation is that they have perished in what they would consider to be good company (16, cf. Isa. **14**.10,11). The reference in vs. 16, 18 to the trees of Eden cannot mean that the actual trees in the garden of Eden are cut down, but that Eden-like trees perish. Similarly, the expression 'ships of Tarshish' came to mean any big ships resembling the large ocean-going vessels that sailed to Tarshish (Isa. **2**.16).

The final reference to the uncircumcised (18) is to those who are outside of the covenant (**28**.10; **32**.21). The term is understandable, though the Bible in other places makes it clear that God is concerned with circumcision of the heart and not simply with physical circumcision, important though this was as the covenant sign (Deut. **10**.16; Jer. **4**.4; Rom. **2**.25–29).

Note other tree pictures in Psa. 1; Jer. 17.6–8.

Ezekiel 32   Death without Glory

Jerusalem has fallen and Ezekiel still continues his prophecies against Egypt (1,17). Naturally, he spoke of many other things during this whole period, but the editor of the Book, whether or not he was Ezekiel himself, has placed this collection in a single group.

Most speakers use illustrations more than once, and in vs. 2–8 there is a repetition of the thought of **29**.3–5. (See notes.) The opening words differ, since here we have Pharaoh's regard for himself as a lion, whereas he is no more than a crocodile stirring up mud and filth. So God will haul him out and throw him on land to be eaten by birds and beasts. The symbolism of the great Day of the Lord comes again (7,8, cf. **30**.3).

Then comes the repetition of the reaction of other countries at

Egypt's fall (9,10, cf. **31**.16), and the mention of Babylon and other great powers as God's agents (11). The symbolism of desolation, an uninhabited and neglected country, indicates the ruin of the empire (13–15). The theme of lamentation for past glory will be taken up by the mourning women (16, cf. **19**.14).

Now follows a dramatic lamentation such as might well be chanted by the mourners (18–32). Note the magnificent repetitions and refrains. Although the passage is printed as prose, it has the effect of poetry.

The lamentation accompanies the funeral (18). Mighty Egypt has gone the way of all flesh (19–21). Each empire, with its ruler, imagines that it has found the secret of immortality, but one follows another to death. Assyria has gone with all her violence (22,23). Elam, once a great power, was absorbed by Persia (24,25). Meshech and Tubal (**27**.13; **38**.2,3), powers to the north, perish in their turn. The Greek Septuagint and the Syriac version omit 'not' in v. 27. But if it is retained, the reference could be to the picture in **39**.11–16 where the hosts of Gog, who was the chief prince of Mesech and Tubal, lie unburied for a long time, whereas other warriors killed in battle were normally buried quickly. Edom (29) and the Phoenician cities (30) perish also. This is the only consolation Pharaoh can find (31, cf. **31**.16). He is in the company of every kind of fallen greatness.

Togetherness may be deadly. We have read here about nations. As individuals we may ponder Psa. 49.10–20.

Questions for further study and discussion on Ezekiel chs. 25–32

1. What can modern business learn from these chapters?
2. What can politicians learn from them?
3. What passages of fear and threat move you most here? Can you get the feeling of something real that is happening?
4. Why is pride especially obnoxious to God and to man? What does the N.T. say about it?
5. Jesus Christ used pictures from nature and experience in Matt. **13**. Which of the objects from which He drew His illustrations are also used in these chapters?
6. Consider how far predictions in these chapters may fairly be regarded as literal, and how far as expressing truth in illustrative terms.

Ezekiel 33   The Present Moment

There are repetitions of two earlier prophecies in vs. 1–20. Ezekiel is once again reminded of his call to be a watchman (1–9, cf. 3.16–21).

Jeremiah also needed a second commissioning in terms very similar to those used at his call (Jer. **15**.19–21, cf. **1**.17–19). We are enthusiastic when the Lord first becomes real to us, but it is not too difficult to lose the vision.

This section rounds off Ezekiel's ministry during the period before the fall of Jerusalem (21,22), and is a reminder that his work is not yet over. Now the fresh exiles and those who were left in Judah, as well as those who had been taken at the same time as Ezekiel, needed further warning.

So Ezekiel first warns his fellow exiles as he had done previously (10–20 cf. ch. **18**). The common opinion was that they had become so involved in their own and their forefathers' sins that they could do nothing to help themselves. So God reminds them that He is concerned with the present moment, and they must be, too. They must not presume on a past good life if they are now drifting into evil. Yet neither must they sink into despair over the past if now they are ready to turn to God in repentance. But would they take the point, or merely look upon Ezekiel as providing a little entertainment for a drab existence (30–33)?

There is a message for those who had eluded the Babylonians (23–29). They were saying that, if Abraham, a single individual, was given the land, how much more would they have it now for themselves. The answer is that they would not escape suffering for the wrongs that characterized them in common with the rest of the nation. The *Book of Lamentations* shows their sufferings.

Now at last comes the news that Jerusalem has fallen (21,22). Ezekiel had experienced one of those periods of dumbness that sometimes preceded a striking message or event (3.26,27, cf. **24**.25–27). Next morning he and his fellow exiles heard the news.

The date in v. 21 is superficially difficult. Jerusalem was captured in the 11th year of Zedekiah's reign and of Jehoiachin's captivity (e.g. Jer. **39**.2; 2 Kings **25**.2), and it is unlikely that the news took nearly 18 months to reach Babylon. It may be that at this point there is a difference between the Palestinian and Babylonian reckoning of the date when the new year began, whether in spring or in autumn. The Greek Septuagint, however, reads 'the eleventh year', which removes the difficulty.

How important is our past?

Ezekiel 34   Shepherds and the Shepherd

Although, as we have seen in ch. **33**, Ezekiel still has the responsibility to warn, he is now set free to talk to his people of what God will do with them and for them after they have learned the lessons of the exile. We must be prepared for a blend of near and distant future, such as we often find in prophecy (1 Pet. 1.10–12). Thus this chapter begins with contemporary bad rulers and ends with the Messiah.

This seems puzzling, but it makes sense. There are certain laws of God that run through history, and yet find their full meaning in the two comings of Jesus Christ. We saw in 30.1–4 that this is true of the judgement of the Day of the Lord; there are lesser days of God's intervention on the way to the Second Coming. Similarly every ruler is intended to be a true shepherd, and every king should be a true David, just as every human being should be truly in the image of God. When we fail, we do not thwart the final purpose of God, however much, from the human standpoint, we appear to have delayed it. God's perfect Man and perfect David has come and will come. Thus a passage about the rulers of God's people inevitably ends with Christ, however many good and bad rulers there may be beforehand.

The comparison of rulers and shepherds comes several times in the prophets (e.g. Isa. 56.11; Jer. 25.34; 50.6; Zech. 10.2,3) and naturally reminds us of Jesus Christ (e.g. Isa. 40.11; Zech. 13.7; John 10.1–7; 1 Pet. 5.3,4). A passage which closely resembles this chapter of *Ezekiel* is Jer. 23.1–6. Note also how, by comparing vs. 15 and 23, we have an underlying hint of the deity of our Lord Jesus Christ.

An additional picture is used in vs. 17–24, comparable to Christ's parable of the sheep and the goats. It is not only the leaders who are at fault, but within the flock there are those who are concerned only with their own interests, and not content with this, are deliberately spoiling life for others. Today one thinks of those who foul literature, stage, screen and television.

The chapter ends with the good rule of the Messiah. The days of the Messiah began with Christ's first coming, and although the Jews did enjoy God's blessing on their return from exile, the language here carries us into the sort of metaphors that the N.T. uses to describe the New Covenant that Jews and Gentiles enjoy in Christ (e.g. John 7.37,38; 15.1–7; Rom. 11.17–24; Gal. 5.22,23).
Consider the Shepherd work of Jesus Christ.

Ezekiel 35   The Opportunist

Ezekiel has already included Edom briefly with other nations that come under the censure of God (25.12–14). Now he is given a longer message. The strong words should be compared with other Edom passages, especially Psa. 137.7; Obad. 8–14; Isa. 34; Jer. 49.7–22; Mal. 1.2–5.

It is strange how the rivalry between Jacob and Esau was perpetuated in their descendants. Isaac was shown by God that there would be this struggle (Gen. 27.39,40), and history records it from time to time (e.g. Num. 20.14–21; 2 Sam. 8.13,14; 2 Kings 8.20–22). Edom thought that eventually Israel would be obliterated, and she joined with the Babylonians in rounding up the refugees and taking what she could by way of spoil. For this she is condemned in vs. 1–9.

The further condemnation (10–15) is for land-grabbing. Now that so many of the people had gone into exile, it might seem that the Lord had left the land completely, and had retired defeated. From one aspect it was true that the Lord had left His Temple and city (11.23), but He had not abandoned His people altogether, and still owned the land (10). The land was not for Edom to take, especially since she supposed that she had defeated or abolished God in taking it (12,13). God was not just an idol attached to a tribe, one who perished when his worshippers perished.

Mount Seir (2) is the name for the northern mountains of Edom, south of the Dead Sea. At some time between this prophecy and Mal. 1.3, Edom's territory was overrun by the Nabataeans. Eventually Edom was conquered and absorbed by the Jews, although ironically the Herods were Idumeans (Edomites). Herod the Great knew the Lord (15) sufficiently to rebuild the Temple from 20 B.C. onwards, although he and his descendants turned their hostility against Christ and the Christians, and once again showed themselves enemies of the people of God.

When did I last take advantage of someone else's misfortunes?

Ezekiel 36.1-21 God's Reputation

This chapter introduces an important principle, for which some have criticised Ezekiel (see also ch. 20), in that God is concerned for His Holy Name (21) rather than with love for His people. It is wrong to set the one against the other. God loves all mankind, but His purpose in choosing Israel was that they might make Him known to the world. Unfortunately they interpreted this choice solely in terms of power, and not of moral and spiritual values. So long as they had the land, the city, and the Temple, and their kings conquered the surrounding nations, they felt that all was well (e.g. Jer. 7.4).

As a result of their behaviour (17) they conveyed the impression that their God was no different from the gods of the nations round about, for whom the word *holy* had no moral significance. The messages of all the prophets were directed towards what it meant to be the people of God, a meaning already contained in the ten commandments. But every prophet was rejected by the nation as a whole, although always there were some who listened.

Thus God had to demonstrate that it mattered more what His people were in themselves than where they lived, and, for the sake of His Name (i.e. His character and reputation), He took them into exile.

Now the situation was different. Many of the exiles were learning the lesson. Yet the pagan peoples were interpreting God's character as though He were powerless to defend and restore Israel (6). So again God acts for His Name's sake.

This section follows on from ch. 35 with the key word 'mountains', although it is obvious from what is said that all the land is included. The word prepares us for a certain amount of symbolism, just as when the Temple is called the mountain of the Lord (Isa. 2.2,3). 'Mountain' in the O.T. sometimes has a mystical sense. Hence we shall see that these promises of return to the land go beyond mere literalism, just as the return from exile in Isa. 40–55 gets its full meaning from the return from the exile of sin which comes through the work of Christ.

Meanwhile the words had a literal fulfilment. The Jews did possess the land again, and it became fruitful.

Check some of the symbolic references to mountains, e.g. Psa. 125. 1,2; Isa. 65.25; Jer. 51.25; Zech. 6.1; Gal. 4.24,25; Heb. 12.22; Rev. 21.10.

Ezekiel 36.22-38 The Gospel Promise

The opening verses clearly bring out the point that God's Name, or reputation, was suffering. It was profaned by the low standards of behaviour, but also by the apparent powerlessness of God to restore His people if they turned to Him in repentance. These verses promise more than a bare return. The people certainly enjoyed the land again, although the Books of *Haggai*, *Zechariah*, and *Malachi* show that they still often fell back, just as the Christian Church has done since Calvary and Pentecost. But certainly the exile implanted in the people as a whole a disgust for idolatry (25).

Verses 26,27 point to the New Covenant and the work of the Holy Spirit based on the finished work of Jesus Christ on the cross. The Old Covenant specifically begins to anticipate the New (e.g. Jer. 31.31–34; Joel 2.28,29). In the New there is the approach from within, where the Spirit comes to take up the transforming control. He could not do this, as He does now, until the redemptive work of

Christ was complete (John **7**.39), even though from time to time in the O.T. He inspired individuals for special tasks (e.g. Exod. **31**.3; Judg. **6**.34; 2 Sam. **23**.2; Ezek. **3**.12).

The terms of the promise in vs. 25–27 show that we are not wrong in looking for symbolic interpretations in these chapters. No one supposes that the reference in v. 25 is to literal water, but Ezekiel speaks of the reality, underlying the ritual sprinklings of the Law, e.g. Num. **19**.17–19; Heb. **9**.10; **10**.22.

It is likely that Christ was calling the attention of Nicodemus to this passage when He spoke in John **3**.5 of the new birth through water and the Spirit; the Ezekiel promise was about to be fulfilled. Paul also speaks of the stone and the heart of flesh in 2 Cor. **3**.3. Note also the inwardness of Jer. **31**.33,34. As Christians we know this new life, and agree with the verdict of v. 32; how could we be saved on the ground of our own achievements and non-achievements?

Meanwhile the returning Jews knew God's power to cleanse (33; Zech. **3**.1–5) even though they had not yet come into the era of the Spirit; and they repeopled the land (34–38).

Study the negative and positive aspects of vs. 24–27—the cleansing and the renewing.

Ezekiel 37.1-14   Life from the Dead

The promises of ch. **36** might well sound incredible to prisoners immersed in the mighty Babylonian power. Once they had been a living and vital organism. Now they were scattered like bones lying stark and dry under the desert sun.

This is how they appear to Ezekiel in his vision. Can they live again? To man it seems impossible, but God knows the answer (3). The answer lies in the word of the Lord (4); that declaration which effects what it promises (Isa. **55**.11).

The resurrection that follows does not refer directly to individual resurrection from death. It is symbolic of the recreation and revitalizing of the nation as a whole, as the interpretation shows (11–14).

Bringing the bones together is only a beginning. Clothing them with muscles and skin is still only a step on the way. The body is still dead, since it lacks the vital breath of life. In what follows it is impossible to be consistent in our translation of the word *ruach*. It is the word that appears in vs. 9 and 14 as 'breath', 'wind', and 'Spirit'. Thus in the Hebrew there is a link that we may miss in English. Nicodemus also was reminded of this in John **3**.8, where the margin points out that in Greek also the word *pneuma* has the double meaning.

This helps us to understand the nature of the new birth. The body needs breath if it is to live. Man has dropped from the life of God through the fall and through personal sin, and the Bible describes our state as death, even though we still have biological life (John 5.24; Rom. 5.15; Col. 2.13). The new birth involves both the removal of sin through the work of Christ, and also the reception of the breath of the Spirit to vitalize and renew us (John 3.5, 14–18). Thus we see the analogy between the natural and the spiritual; what is true at one level is true at the other also.

The picture is applicable both to individual and to Church life. Humanism has to stop with v. 8. So do many schemes for unity within the visible Church. Naturally we want the visible 'body' to be as tidy as possible, without any limbs missing, but we may forget the prime importance of the Holy Spirit. The Bible does not teach that the Holy Spirit is in every man, but that He comes in to make alive.

Consider some analogies between the Holy Spirit and breath.

Ezekiel 37.15-28 Nations United

We must decide what is the proper interpretation of the uniting of the two kingdoms. The Northern Kingdom of Israel was taken captive to northern Mesopotamia in 721 B.C. The Southern Kingdom of Judah was taken to southern Mesopotamia in 586 B.C. There was no mass return of Israel comparable to the return of Judah, and the so-called 'lost tribes' have by some been identified with peoples who moved across Europe into Britain, and Biblical promises to Israel are applied to them.

Ezekiel takes two sticks, with the name of Judah and associated tribes on one, and the name of Ephraim, the son of Joseph, and the largest of the northern tribes, with its associated tribes, on the other. He then puts the sticks end to end and folds his hand over the join, so that they appear as one. The meaning is drawn out as union in the land, with 'David' ruling over both, with a special covenant, and with the presence of God in His sanctuary among them.

We must remember that very many Israelites remained in Palestine. Some have calculated that only 1 in 20 were taken away. Both Hezekiah and Josiah, after the Northern captivity, summoned those who remained to come to the Passover (2 Chron. 30; 34.9; 35.17,18). After the return of the Jews, distinction was made between semi-pagan Israelites who had been mixed with the imported colonists (Ezra 4.1–3), and those who made a clean break with paganism (Ezra **6**.21). Thus, the two peoples were united, and it would also be most improbable if some Israelite exiles from Mesopotamia did not join in the return of their Jewish kinsmen, although their longer period in exile had attached them more closely to their new homes. Later the two divided again into Jews and Samaritans.

However, the promise here, as in Jer. **33**.14–26, is linked to the days of the Messiah. This is the N.T. truth that Jews and Samaritans are all one in Christ (Acts **8**.4–17), and also that Gentiles are equally one with them (Gal. **3**.28,29). We note also Christ's words to the Samaritan woman about the unity of worship (John **4**.19–26). Even the actual land (25) becomes unimportant. Jerusalem on earth was sacramental of Jerusalem above, of which Jews, Israelites, and Gentiles are citizens in Christ (Gal. **4**.26; Heb. **12**.22). And we, too, enjoy the everlasting covenant (26; Matt. **26**.28).

Compare what is said here about reunion in the Messiah with Jer. 31 (note v. 31) and Hos. 3.4,5, and note the marginal references in v. 27.

Questions for further study and discussion on Ezekiel chs. 33–37

1. Is it every Christian's duty to be a watchman?
2. Must the Christian watchman warn *everyone*? If not, how does he know whom to warn?
3. In the light of **33**.32, should a preacher aim at being a good speaker?
4. What light do these chapters throw on the Messiah?
5. What do these chapters say about salvation from sin?

Ezekiel 38.1-13   The Last Battle

This is the first of a series of chapters on which most commentators would admit that they cannot speak with any certainty. In this chapter we have to ask: When does the attack take place? Who are the people concerned? How much is literal and how much symbolic?

The N.T. has a reference to this passage, where, in Rev. **20**.7–9, at the end of the Millennium Satan gathers 'the nations which are at the four corners of the earth, that is, Gog and Magog' and attacks 'the camp of the saints and the beloved city.' The present commentator believes in a literal reign of Christ on earth with His people (not only Jews), and so is inclined to place the *Ezekiel* passage at the end of this period, during which there will be universal peace and dropping of armaments (11).

Others regard the Millennium of Rev. **20** as picturing the present rule of Christ during the gospel age, with the power of Satan potentially broken. At the end of this era there will be a heading up of evil and a final attack on all the people of God. There is much in Scripture to indicate that there will be such an outburst before the Lord returns (e.g. 2 Thes. **2**.3,4; Rev. **16**.12–16), and even those who believe in an earthly Millennium commonly accept this, and may think of another Gog and Magog attack at this time.

Others who believe in a great national future for the Jews take this chapter as an attack on the land of Israel, either at the end of a period of tribulation before the Lord returns, or at the end of the Millennium.

In any case we must somehow link this chapter with Joel **3** and Zech. **14**, which also describe a great attack on Jerusalem, during which the Lord appears to overthrow the enemy.

Of the peoples named here, several occur in ch. **27** (see notes). Those in v. 2 are in the north, Persia (5) is east, and Cush and Put are south. Gomer (6) is the name for the Cimmerians in Cappadocia, and so are to the west. Thus the enemy comes from all quarters (Rev. **20**.8).

The name Gog is otherwise unknown, but he comes from the land of Magog (2), who is linked with some of these other names in Gen. **10**.2.

God threatens the attackers with defeat (3,4), but foretells that their attack will not come until the distant future (7). God's people will be dwelling quietly (11) at the centre of the earth (12). Traders from Arabia and distant Tarshish come to make a profit out of the war (13), as already happens today.

The LAST battle. What a wonderful adjective!

Ezekiel 38.14-23   Challenge to Antichrist

Gog is the leader, and swoops down from the north (15), although we have seen that his allies come from all points of the compass. It is striking that God says He will bring the invader (16). On other occasions when God brings the invader, it is to punish His people (e.g. ch. **21**), but this is for the final overthrow of evil, and the consequent vindication of God's good Name. If this is Satan's last attempt to rally the world against God (Rev. **20**.7–10), his defeat is the day for which all creation has waited since the Fall.

There is a strange challenge in v. 17. God asserts in a rhetorical question that Gog is the heading up of all that the prophets have spoken concerning 'antichrists'. In the O.T. there were proud defiers of God (e.g. Isa. **10**.7–19; **14**.12–20) even when they were for a time God's instruments of punishment. Since the address to

Gog was far in the future when Ezekiel spoke, we may include the prophecies of Dan. **11**, Christ's words in Matt. **24**.15, and Paul's words in 2 Thess. **2**.3,4.

The invaders are destroyed by earthquake (19,20, cf. Zech. **14**.4,5), by violent distrust of one another (21, cf. Zech. **14**.13), by pestilence (22, cf. Zech. **14**.12), and by torrential rain and fire from heaven (22, cf. Rev. **20**.9). The end result is the vindication of God and the recognition by everyone of His sole Godhead (23).

This is, after all, the ultimate purpose of creation, the sole glory of God. It is wrought through history, through the incarnation and the work of Jesus Christ, and rounded off by the second coming and all that goes with it (Phil. **2**.5–11). It would be a happy thing if all could be achieved through love alone, but experience and Scripture show that love has been abused and resisted. We do not like to think of the judgements of God, but ultimately the great Surgeon cuts away the cancer that clamours for its right to dominate the body.

Surely God must one day vindicate and be vindicated. Mal. 3.13–4.3.

Ezekiel 39.1-16   Armaments and Bones

It seems likely that this chapter is a second sermon on the invasion, and thus vs. 1–6 form a brief recapitulation of ch. 38. God brings the host of invaders, renders them powerless, and destroys them. The result is the full vindication of God, the final summing up of the purpose of creation, the day towards which all prophecy points (8).

The emphasis now is not on destruction, but rather on the removal of every trace of rebellion and sin. If the invasion is literal, and centred on the land of Israel, then all that is said about the removal of its traces must be literal, too. Thus the weapons of war are completely burnt up (9,10), and the bones of the rebellious dead are taken across the Jordan and buried in a valley east of the Dead Sea, so that the Holy Land is no longer contaminated by them either in fact or in reminder.

The valley may be in the Mountains of Abarim (11, margin), which are east of the northern end of the Dead Sea. The bones buried there will be so many that they block the way through the valley (11), or perhaps the block is a moral ban on going through such a polluted place.

The removal of the bones is comparatively easy at first, and everyone takes part (13). After seven months all obvious traces will have been removed, so a group of investigators is appointed to finish the work (14). Ordinary people still help by calling attention to to any bones that they find (15). There is no known city of Hamonah (16), but if a valley is to be called Hamon-gog, there could also be a near-by city with a somewhat similar name.

A literal interpretation, which puts these events at the end of the Millennium (Rev. 20.7–10), would indicate that there is still a period of life on earth before the ushering in of eternity.

Meanwhile the spiritual trend of this section is towards the abolition of armaments. The abandoned weapons are not to be used again, but must be totally burned. They do not form part of the spoil that may be kept (9,10; Isa. 9.5). Also all traces of the rebellion must go. Today our towns and cities are full of contaminating bones that reek of moral decay, and ordinary people and experts are unable to clear them out of the land.

Can we bury a bone today? Gal. 5.19–21.

Ezekiel 39. 17-29 — Death and Discipline

The previous section spoke of burying bones. Certainly it would not be easy to remove so many corpses to a valley beyond the Dead Sea. Now it appears that birds and beasts first flock to the battle-field to feed on the bodies of the slain. The reference in v. 18 does not mean that large numbers of animals will be killed with the invaders, but, as v. 19 indicates, the picture is that of a great sacrifice, where the bodies of Gog's host are the equivalent of sheep and bulls (cf. Rev. 19.17,18).

This metaphor of the Lord's sacrifice is both strange and repugnant to our ways of thinking, but it occurs also in Isa. 34.5–7; Jer. 46.10; Zeph. 1.7–9. There is no suggestion in these passages that people are sacrificed to appease the Lord, though there is the implication that the Lord cannot rest until all sin is removed. Rather, the metaphor is drawn from what all Israelites could picture. Very few of us in England have ever seen an abattoir, or slaughter-house, or watched the ritual slaughter of animals, so it would be useless to use them as an illustration of blood pouring everywhere. But every Israelite had watched the blood flowing at the sacrifices. This was not pointless slaughter, since most sacrifices were eaten by the worshippers after they had been offered. They provided the fairly infrequent occasions when the average man had a meat meal. But here the quantities of blood that flowed at the sacrifices are used pictorially of the death of those who have campaigned against God.

The vindication of God is seen as much more than the destruction of His enemies. It is seen in the history of His discipline of His people (21–29). This is of vital importance to us who read these

60

chapters. We can stand at a distance and thank God that we are not in Gog's army. But God is even more concerned about His Israel. History shows that not only the Jews were sent into exile to emerge in greater purity, but churches also, who have grown prosperous and forgetful of God and His real claims, have gone down before their enemies. In their captivity a nucleus of faithful believers has risen again.

At the end of time we shall understand and approve God's dealings with all His people. Rev. 15.3,4.

Ezekiel 40.1-16   The Way In

The closing chapters describe a temple in great detail. It does not correspond to the one that was built after the return, nor to Herod's Temple. Some therefore hold that it has yet to be built, and that it will be a centre of worship for the Israeli nation.

This commentary is based on the belief that the visionary temple is intended to be symbolic. It seems unlikely that God will reintroduce animal sacrifices (**43**.18–27) after all that is said in *Hebrews* about their abolition through the sacrifice of Jesus Christ. It seems unlikely that the miraculous river flowing from the temple (**47**) is literal. Moreover the section is introduced as a vision on a high mountain with 'a structure like a city' near by (**40**.2). The words suggest a three-dimensional picture. Therefore, just as Heb. 9 finds a permanent message in the structure of the Tabernacle, so we must look for the significant elements in this vision of the city and temple, noting how it portrays the character of God, the manner of approach to Him, and our way of life as the people of God.

The date is 572 B.C. Ezekiel, like Jesus Christ in His temptation, is taken to the top of a very high mountain (2; Matt. **4**.8). Jesus was shown the glory of the world. Ezekiel is shown the community of God. He is given a shining heavenly guide, who carries a measuring rod of about 10 feet 4 inches. (The so-called 'long cubit' of v. 5 was 20.679 inches, as opposed to the ordinary cubit of about 17.5 inches.)

The guide measures the temple area, just as in Rev. **21**.15–17 John's guide measures the heavenly city. It is not easy to follow the description without a plan, but the essentials are as follows. The outer court is square, with a central gate in the wall on each side at the top of a flight of steps (5,6). The gate is like a college gate at some universities, with side rooms for the guards, and a further porch with side posts (jambs) leading into the court (7–11). The side rooms had something built up in front of their entrances (12), possibly for the guards to stand on. The doors of the side rooms were at the back, opening into the court. Light was admitted through a series of windows, like the slits in old castles but widening outwards instead of inwards (16).

We cannot find a spiritual significance in every measurement, but we note the symmetry of the temple and its precincts (cf. Rev. 21.16).

The approach to God is through a narrow gateway (Matt. 7.13; John 10.1.).

Ezekiel 40.17-49   Approach to the Temple

Ezekiel passes through the eastern gateway into the outer court (17). A raised pavement, level with the inside of the gate, runs round the inside of the walls, with thirty rooms opening on to it (17,18). These rooms would be for the use of the Levites and others who serve in the outer court. If we picture the inner court as a square in the centre of the outer court, the distance between the outer and the inner gates is 100 cubits (19).

There are also similar gates in the north wall of the outer court (19–23) and in the south (24–27). There is no similar gate on the west, since the inner court, in the exact centre of the outer court, opened westwards into the temple, and this led on to the west wall.

Next Ezekiel goes up by eight steps to the south gate of the inner court (28–30). Its dimensions are the same as the outer gates, and as the inner gates on the east (32–34) and north (35–37). The north gate had a special room for the preparation of the offerings (38–43).

There were two extra rooms just inside the inner court by the north and south gates, the former for the priests who had a general ministry in the temple, and the other for the priests of the family of Zadok, who had special responsibilities for the sacrifices at the altar (44–46). The inner court was 100 cubits square, the same measurement as the distance across from the outer to the inner gates.

At last Ezekiel comes to the actual temple (48,49). He had ascended steps into the outer (**40**.6) and inner (**40**.31) courts, and now he ascends ten more into the vestibule. On either side were two pillars, either to support the structure, or corresponding to the two pillars in Solomon's Temple. The meaning of these is uncertain, but their names Jachin and Boaz (1 Kings 7.21) may well have been the first words of two texts inscribed on them, e.g. '*He will establish* thy throne' and '*In the strength* of the Lord I will rejoice'. The words would be a special reminder to the king, and perhaps he stood by them at his coronation (2 Kings 11.14).

We cannot go further than the outer court—without Christ.

*Ezekiel 41.1-11   The Heart of the Temple

Ezekiel passes through the porch into the temple itself. The RSV uses the word *nave* of the larger room within the temple. The measurements of v. 1 are those of the entrance through the wall from the porch to the temple; the wall is six cubits thick. The width of the entrance is ten cubits, and, once one passes through, there are five cubits of wall on each side, thus making a total breadth of twenty cubits (2).

Both courts are exact squares, but the temple is rectangular (2), directing the attention towards the end, where was the inner room, or holy of holies. Ezekiel as a priest could go into the nave, but only the high priest could enter the inner room. Thus he records that the angel alone went in and announced the dimensions (3,4). The inner room is exactly square (4). Its height is not given, but it may have been a cube, as in Solomon's Temple (1 Kings 6.20).

The description of the side rooms (5–11) is difficult to follow. They were probably used to store gifts and tithes and various temple vessels (cf. Neh. 13.5,9,12). They were built on a raised strip on the north and south of the temple, i.e. along the length of it (8). The temple wall narrowed at each storey to form a shelf, or offset, on which each higher room could be supported. This made the rooms a little wider as they rose. There were thirty rooms on each of three floors, and they were reached by a stairway.

They could not be entered from inside the temple, but they opened on to the platform. The implication of v. 11 is that there was only one door in the centre of each side, and the stairway must have started from there.

'The chambers of the court' (10) are those described in ch. 42. There is a space between them and the edge of the temple platform. They are on the north and south (the long sides) of the temple.

Psalm 84.4,10.

*Ezekiel 41.12-26   Inner Beauty

The west side of the temple was different from the others, in that across the pavement there was another building, which ran up to the western wall of the outer court (12). It was set broadways on to the end of the temple. No indication of its use is given, but presumably it was for storage. The distance from the west end of the temple to the west wall, taking in this other building, was equal to the length of the temple itself, i.e. about 174 feet (13). The measurement across the front of the temple (14) is the total width of the inner court (**40**.47), on to which the temple opened. Similarly, behind the temple, the extra building, with wall space on either side, occupied the same length as the inner court (15). Thus the inner court, the temple, and the extra building, with the rooms and walls attached to them, formed a rectangle running up to the western wall of the outer court.

Like Solomon's Temple, this one was panelled throughout (15,16). Nothing is said about the roof, but obviously this temple had one, since windows were needed for light and air. It is not clear how the windows were covered (16), but perhaps they had shutters to keep out storms. Ezekiel could see that the panelling ran as far as the outside of the entrance to the holy of holies (17), but he was not allowed to see whether it ran into the inner room.

The walls were covered with wood carvings of cherubim and palm trees (17–20). Solomon's Temple also had these, together with flower motifs (1 Kings **6**.29). These cherubim, being carved against the flat wood, had only two of their faces depicted, whereas in his opening vision Ezekiel had seen four (**1**.10).

Ezekiel had already seen the altar of burnt-offering in the inner court (**40**.47). Now he is shown a table standing in front of the entrance to the holy of holies (21,22). This is for the showbread (Exod. **25**.23–30).

There were double doors at the entrance to the temple and to the holy of holies (23,24), and the former had the same carvings as on the walls (25).

Cherubim reminded the priests of attendance in the service of God. Palm trees reminded of strength and nourishment (dates) for man (Psalm 92.12–14).

Ezekiel 42   Rooms Set Apart

Opposite to the long sides of the temple, and level with the walls of the inner court, there were rooms for the priests. They were in three storeys, built against the outer court (3). A long corridor divided them into two blocks, and the doors of the southern block opened into this corridor (4). If the other doors also opened north (4), there must have been room for a way between the rooms and the outer court in addition to the inner corridor. Each set of rooms was narrower than the one below, so as to leave a gallery, on to which presumably the rooms on the first and second floors opened (5,6).

The block that faced the temple took up twice the length of the block facing the outer court (8), and the extra space was made up by a wall (7). There was an entrance at the east on the corner that touched the outer court (9,10,14).

Separation is an important theme in these chapters which emphasise the majesty and holiness of God. In pre-exilic times Canaanite influence had degraded the true character of God, as we saw in chs. 8 and 9 and there was little sense of man's sin as he came before God (Isa. 1.4,11–17).

In these rooms the priests are to eat their portions of the sacrifices that have been dedicated to God (13, cf. 44.28–31). What has been given to God is separated to be used as He shows; we cannot take it back again as we wish. Moreover the priests must wear special clothes when they are functioning as priests in the temple (14). God and man are separate, and until the time of Christ only a privileged class could serve in the temple. The clothes spoke of separation to God from the dirt and dust of ordinary life.

The whole temple area forms a square, measuring nearly 300 yards on each side (15–19). Once again a wall marks off the sacred from the secular (20).

What significance is there in symmetry? Cf. Rev. 21.15,16.

Questions for further study and discussion on Ezekiel chs. 38—42

1. What other passages of Scripture indicate special attacks on the people of God in the last days?
2. Is it relevant to these passages that the Israelis have now returned to the Holy Land?
3. Draw a sketch map of the Temple.
4. Think of some buildings, rooms, or open spaces of approximately the areas mentioned in these temple chapters. One cubit is 20.67 inches, three about five feet, 100 about 60 yards.

Ezekiel 43   First Things First

The temple is useless without the presence of God. It is like a man, made in the image of God, without the Holy Spirit. In an earlier vision (11.22,23) Ezekiel had seen the glory of God departing. Now the Lord returns into the temple, while the prophet remains in the inner court (4,5).

God's voice from the temple describes this as His throne, the centre where His presence is focused, as we can focus the sun on one spot with a magnifying glass without making it leave 'heaven'. If His presence is to remain, the old separating evils must go. God mentions the immoralities of ch. 22, but adds the evils that had come from the royal palace being virtually within the temple area (7,8). The reference to the dead bodies (7) may be to burials or to monuments (margin) in proximity to the temple. In Manasseh's reign certainly all sorts of desecration had occurred (2 Kings 21.1–9).

Just as God first declared His law to the Israelites before He made the covenant (Exod. 24.3), so now He first describes the way of separateness and approachability (10–12). It is not surprising that He starts with the altar of burnt-offering in the centre of the inner court (13, cf. 40.47). We too can approach God only through the blood shed on the altar of the cross.

The altar has a square base one cubit deep, with a rim on top. The words in brackets (13) mean that this is the long cubit (40.5). On this base rests a smaller square two cubits high. Another smaller square rests on this and supports the actual hearth, which, like the square, is four cubits deep. There are horns on each of the four corners.

Each square, being smaller than the one below, has a step one cubit wide all round. The total height of the altar, including the horns, is twelve cubits, or some 20½ feet. Although steps ran all round, they were too deep for the robed priests to use, so on the east side they were filled in with steps of normal size, so that the priests faced the temple when they sacrificed (13–17). The blood was smeared on the horns (20), and people seeking sanctuary could seize them (e.g. 1 Kings 1.50).

Even our holiest efforts are mixed with impurities, and the work of our hands, even an altar built for God, needs to be 'decontaminated' (26). All sacrifices in the O.T. anticipate the final sacrifice of Christ, so the three chief sacrificial animals are offered here (18–27).

Heb. 9.22–24.

*Ezekiel 44.1-16   Faithful and Unfaithful

Ezekiel is brought to the east gate of the outer court (1), through which he has seen the glory of God streaming in (43.1–4). Now it remains for ever shut (1,2). This reminds us that none can go the same atoning way by which Christ went into the heavenly temple (Heb. 9.11–14). The prince, who in some points also typifies the Messiah, does not go through the gate again, but enjoys the oneness of fellowship with God there (3).

Instead of returning to the inner court by the obvious way, Ezekiel is taken by way of the north gate. The reason appears in 46.1, i.e. the east gate was opened only on the sabbath.

God has spoken of the holiness of the temple things; now He speaks of the holiness of the people who use them. It is clear from vs. 5–8 that in the last days of Solomon's Temple the priests had allowed anyone, even uncovenanted pagans, to act as priests and temple servants. Either they had been lazy or busy with their own affairs, and had hired others to do their work; or they had taken bribes from pagans who wanted to serve in the Temple, perhaps for the offerings that they were able to take home and resell.

To understand vs. 10–14, we note that the family of Levi had different functions. Most were temple servants, but those who were descended from Aaron were priests in the temple (e.g. Num. 8.20–26). These verses deal with the latter group (13). They had previously countenanced idolatry, and now they are to be degraded to the level of the other Levites.

The new priesthood is confined to the line of Zadok, who was a descendant of Eleazar, the third son of Aaron. Representatives of this line had evidently stood firm (15,16). Even though this visionary temple was not built after the return, the line of Zadok continued to hold the high priesthood until 171 B.C..

God has not given my work for others to do.

*Ezekiel 44.17-31 Good Servants of God

At first sight these regulations for the priests seem strange, but by analysing them we shall find that some are practical, and others have a general application to us as Christians, since we are all priests (Rev. 1.6).

Linen clothes were worn because the priests could easily become too hot through the fire on the altar. The smell of perspiration can be unpleasant, and this suggests a lesson in personal hygiene (17,18). The idea of communicating holiness (19) is that any close experience of God set a person or thing apart. Anyone who treated him or it lightly, violated this set-apartness, which was communicated to them in a wrong way.

Their hair style must not follow extreme fashions to conform to current religious or social customs (20). They must be in full control of their faculties so as to offer intelligent worship to God, not using drink (or drugs?) to release their inhibitions (21, cf. Prov. 31.4,5). They must have a good wife. She must not have been divorced, or even a widow who had become used to a very different form of life than that which she would have as the wife of a priest (22).

The laws of clean and unclean are mostly commonsense. They show that in food (e.g. Deut. 14.3–21) and in hygiene (e.g. Lev. 13.9–17; Deut. 23.12–14) God is concerned for the well-being of the whole person.

The priests are to have the wisdom to act as judges, but they must be very different from the sort of judges that the prophets denounce (e.g. Isa. **1**.23). They themselves must be under the judgement of God in their observance of the worship (24).

Some of the Mosaic laws were designed to cover risks which would not always be present. Thus anyone who had contact with a dead body had to be isolated as unclean for fear of infection, and then be formally, as well as practically, cleansed with water and with a sin offering (Num. **19**.11–22). We conclude that the offering was a reminder that death came into the human race because of sin. The priests may have contact with close relatives who have died; God does not discourage reasonable mourning (25–27, cf. **24**.17).

The priests earn their living by doing the special work that God has given them, and their income comes from the offerings (28–30). God still calls some to what we call wholetime service, and in giving for their support we are giving to God, as were the people who brought their offerings to the Temple (1 Cor. **9**.13,14).

Finally, the priests must not risk infection from eating tainted meat (31).

How do these rules apply to us?

Ezekiel 45 Just and Righteous

Ezekiel has described the temple and the laws for the priests, using the third person. Now he directly addresses various sections of the community. Even though this temple and city are visionary, the restored Israelites must learn the principles that must govern what they actually do.

The princes (8,9) are to mark out the land in a way that safeguards the separateness of God. There is to be a reserved area of something like eight miles (east to west) by seven (1). In the centre there is the temple area, already measured in **42**.15–20, of some 300 yards square, with an unoccupied strip of about thirty yards around it (2).

Next a rectangle is measured off, running the full length from east to west, and containing the temple area (3). Thus this strip is approximately eight miles by three and a half, and is for the priests' homes. A similar strip for the Levites adjoins it on the north (5). On the south a strip half the width is for the city, containing houses and park land (6, cf. **48**.15); this, added to the sacred rectangular portion, forms a square.

Just as priest and sacrifice represent Christ and His offering, and yet need reapplication to Christ Himself, so also does the prince as the completely righteous Messianic ruler. His person and actions are relevant for us if they are reapplied. Thus, in vs. 7,8 his possessions run right across the land, including both sacred and secular areas.

Other princes rule with him (cf. Rev. **1.**6; Eph. **2.**6), and are to be like him in their love of righteousness (8,9). For example, they are to ensure proper standards of honesty. Traders must give full measure, with the bath of 5¾ gallons for liquids, and with thee phah which was the equivalent dry measure. The homer is ten times the capacity. The shekel is about 11.39 grams or 0.402 oz. (10–12). See also Lev. **19.**35,36 and Amos **8.**5 for examples of short measure for purchases and heavy weights to weigh the buyer's silver.

The offerings of each person are proportionate to his earnings, and are one-sixtieth of cereals, one hundredth of oil, and one-two hundredth of sheep. These offerings are accepted as atoning for sin (13–15). Cereal and vegetable offerings commonly accompanied the animal sacrifices, which were atoning because of the shed blood (**46.**5; Num. **15.**1–10). The prince is responsible for collecting the offerings (16,17). He would have the authority that the priests might lack (e.g. Neh. **13.**10–13).

Even the temple needs to be 'cleansed' once a year (18,19, cf. Heb. **9.**23) because its ministers are human and sinful, and even though they have kept from deliberate sin, there is much that contaminates (20, cf. Psa. **19.**12). All leads to the great Passover festival of redemption (21–24), and to the Feast of Tabernacles six months later (25), when the harvest has been gathered in (Lev. **23.**39–42).

Separation, sin, atonement, righteousness; what is the relation between them?

Ezekiel 46 Festivals and Offerings

The sabbath and the first day of each month are marked by the opening of the east gate of the inner court (1). The prince passes through the porch, and from there watches the priests offering the sacrifices on the altar in the centre of the inner court (2). Neither he nor the people actually enters this court. To ensure reverence, there are two lines of worshippers coming to the entrances to watch the offerings, each moving in one direction only (9,10).

The burnt offering (4) was entirely consumed by fire on the altar, picturing the entire offering of Christ on the cross. The offerer identified himself with the animal, which then died in his place (Lev. **1.**4). From the accompanying cereal offering (5) a handful was burned to signify its acceptance by the Lord, while the remainder was given to the priests (Lev. **2.**1–3). The good things that God gives are to be enjoyed in the context of redemption.

Although the turn of each week and each month is marked for cleansing and dedication, the prince is encouraged to come on other occasions with freewill and peace offerings (12), and, while for some of the offerings he and his people have a minimum of accompaniments prescribed, they are told sometimes to search their hearts and make their decision about how much to give (11, cf. 1 Cor. **16**.2).

Whether or not the prince attends, he provides the daily burnt offering, thus putting every day, as well as every week and month, under the cross (13–15).

His gifts are not only to God, but may be to his sons and to his servants as a reward for faithfulness (16–18). His land stretches across Palestine, so he has plenty to spare. People with great possessions are not always generous, and in the old days kings and rulers had sometimes dispossessed their subjects to reward themselves or their favourites (18, cf. Mic. **2**.2). Members of the royal family may keep the land and hand it on; others may hold it only until the year of liberty, which came every fifty years (Lev. **25**.10).

If Ezekiel has not moved since he stood in front of the temple in **44**.4, he now goes into the outer court, and round to the entrance to the priests' rooms (19, cf. **42**.9). Here the priests ate most of the guilt offering and sin offering (20; Lev. **6**.24–7.7). The people ate most of each peace offering (Lev. **7**.11–18,28–36), and these must be what were cooked in the enclosures at each corner of the outer court (21–24). We cannot participate in the atoning aspect of the death of Christ, but we must be personally linked with Him in His death (Rom. **6**).

How far may a sacrifice be a substitute?

*Ezekiel 47.1-12   Living Waters

The pictures in the vision have been built up gradually. Ezekiel had not been shown the river when previously he had stood at the door of the temple, but now he is shown how the presence of God at the centre means life for the barren land. The stream begins as a trickle, coming out from the south-east of the temple, flowing past the south side of the altar of burnt-offering, and out under the south wall. Ezekiel goes out of the north gate, and past the closed east gate, until he comes to the stream, which soon turns towards the Dead Sea (1–3).

He is told to step into these living waters. After just over one-third of a mile the water is up to his ankles. Another third, and it reaches his knees. After about a mile it rises to his waist. Then, only a mile and a third from its source, the waters form a deep river

(3–5). Ezekiel walks back (6), and is struck by the number of trees on the banks (7). The river flows into the Arabah depression, in which lies the Dead Sea (8). Wherever it goes, it freshens the salt and stagnant waters, so that fishermen can make a living along the west shore of the Dead Sea (9,10).

Yet its course is selective, and the valuable chemical salts are unaffected (11). The trees on the bank share the everlasting life which has its source in the temple, and they bear fresh fruit continually, and supply healing medicines in their leaves (12).

This is almost certainly the Scripture that Christ had in mind in John 7.38. His words must be understood in the light of the truth that our bodies become temples of the Holy Spirit (John 7.39; 1 Cor. 6.19). The Spirit in the depth of the temple of our being flows out into a dead world.

From another aspect the picture in this chapter is taken up in the view of the New Jerusalem in Rev. 22.1,2, and it also rounds off the picture of the living waters which flowed from Eden (Gen. 2.10). In between we have reminders that flowing streams are parables of the flowing life of God (e.g. Psa. 42.1; Jer. 2.13; John 4.10–15).

'Everything will live where the river goes' (9). *Meditate on this* (*Isa. 44.3; 58.10,11; Psa. 46.4,5*).

*Ezekiel 47.13—48.20   The Holy Land

It is not possible to identify all the places that form the boundaries of the land (13–20). The western border is naturally the Mediterranean (15,20). The northern border starts opposite Cyprus, and runs across to Hamath and to some unidentified places on the boundary of the former territories owned by Hamath and Damascus (15–17). From there the eastern border runs down into the Jordan valley to a place south of the Dead Sea (18). Then it turns west and runs to the Brook of Egypt, which is a small river on the curve of the coast (19).

This is the area which God swore to give to the nation (14, cf. Gen. 15.18–21; Num. 34.1–12), and which was ruled by Solomon (1 Kings 4.24). In the plan for the future this is divided equally among the tribes, whatever their size, in strips from east to west. It is noteworthy that, although the Book warns against contamination of the temple by aliens (44.6–9), it welcomes foreigners who have been integrated into the nation, thus anticipating the equality of Jews and Gentiles in the Christian Church (22; Eph. 2.11–22).

The tribal territory starts with Dan in the north, and runs south to Judah (48.1–7). Then comes the sacred area already described in

71

45.1–8. The main additions to the description are details about the city and its surroundings (15–20). The city is about a mile and a half square (16), with an open space on each side (17), and land for cultivation to the east and west (18,19). This whole area is regarded as the Lord's property, held in trust for Him (8,20).

How can something belong to God as a holy portion, and still be for our use?

Ezekiel 48.21-35   God is Central

The prince's land (21,22) has already been described in **45.7,8.** The remaining tribes have their territories south of the city. Finally the city is· given three gates on each side, named after the tribes (30–34, cf. Rev. **21.**12,13). One is named after Levi (31) whose territory was separated from that of the twelve tribes, and who consequently was not counted in the twelve strips in **48.**1–7,23–28. Hence the two Joseph tribes, Manasseh and Ephraim (4,5) have one Joseph gate (32) to form the twelve.

The Book ends magnificently. In the N.T. it corresponds to Emmanuel, *God with us* (Matt. **1.**23), and to the Holy Spirit dwelling with us and in us (John **14.**17).

'The Lord is there.' How?

This commentary on the new city and temple has not been exciting, but has tried to explain the main points of the description, so that the reader can follow the outline intelligently. Yet we have regarded these visions as intentionally symbolic, setting out permanent truths in O.T. description, and we have noticed applications that are found in the N.T. Thus the brief description of the New Jerusalem in Rev. **21** and **22** has features in common with these chapters, including measurements, and we do not take them literally. Some of them already operate in the Church, although we do not yet see them in their final form. Thus we enjoy the light of God, the benefits of the tree of life and the water of life, and we serve God as those who are marked with His Name (Rev. **21.**22–**22.**5).

Judah and Israel were physically blessed after the return. They rebuilt the temple, and by the time of Christ, even though they were under Rome, they had absorbed the nations that once harassed them, such as Edom and the Philistines, and had full freedom to practise their religion. Yet their history combined both renewal and apostasy. Malachi shows that God's standards were not always observed, and there were many apostates and bitter struggles for the high priesthood, especially during the 2nd century B.C.

Similarly, the Christian Church has known both revival and apostasy, yet God's promises of victory in Christ have not been overthrown. The Jewish nation as a whole was not ready to move into the New Jerusalem and New Temple of the Messiah when He came. Thus they lost the inner reality of the O.T. promises made through Ezekiel and others. We in the Church have inherited these realities, but we must not ignore the warnings that form the other side of the coin.

Questions for further study and discussion on Ezekiel chs. 43–48

1. What is the value, and what is the danger, of separating the sacred from the secular?
2. Having decided this in general, what particular applications are there to our day-to-day lives?
3. How far am I identified with Christ in His death, and how far is His sacrifice unique? How is this indicated in the sacrifices mentioned in these chapters?
4. If you think it profitable, compare the 'furniture' of this temple with that of the Tabernacle and Solomon's Temple. Some things are not mentioned here, e.g. the altar of incense.

Daniel

INTRODUCTION

The Book falls into two main sections: chs. 1–7 are narratives of Daniel and his three friends; chs. 8–12 are a series of visions of the future. A further division, which does not coincide with the former, is the section 2.4–7.28, which is in Aramaic, while the rest of the Book is in Hebrew. Aramaic is a Semitic language, and was widely used as an international means of communication in the Near East. By the time of Christ it had superseded Hebrew as the popular language of Palestine. No theory of the language switch in *Daniel* has commanded universal acceptance. Perhaps the whole Book was translated from Hebrew into Aramaic, and later one section of the Hebrew was lost; as there was no other copy, the lost section was replaced by the Aramaic translation.

The Book professes to be by Daniel (12.4), and, although objections have been raised to this, our commentary will assume that there are good reasons for taking the Book at its face value. We shall not argue about the objections, but, without ignoring any major difficulty, we shall show how they may be integrated into our understanding of the text.

The Hebrew Bible does not include *Daniel* in the section of the Prophets, perhaps because the style of visions that God gave him was so different from normal prophecy. However, the Lord Jesus Christ referred to him as a prophet, and looked for the fulfilment of what he wrote (Matt. **24.**15).

Daniel 1 Under Test

After Nebuchadnezzar had broken Egypt's hold on Palestine at the battle of Carchemish in 605 B.C., he moved south, and, according to the historian Berossus, he took prisoners from the major states, including Judah. 'The third year' (1) is Babylonian reckoning; Jer. **46.**2 gives 'the fourth year' by Jewish reckoning. Probably Jehoiakim was taken to Babylon for a short time, as Manasseh had been (2; 2 Chron. **36.**6; **33.**10–13), and was exhibited in the temple of Marduk.

Assyrian and Babylonian kings appreciated merit, and here the King selected Daniel and his three friends for special training with a view to becoming members of the class of wise advisers at the royal court. They were renamed, as Joseph had been, in Gen. **41.**45. *Belteshazzar* probably means *Protect his life*, or, shall we say, *Lifeguard? Abednego* is usually taken as *Servant of Nebo*. As Nebo was a Babylonian god, the four friends would not have cared to use the name among themselves. The meanings of *Shadrach* and *Meshach* are unknown.

Daniel emerges as the leader (8–10). He was unsuccessful with the head man (10), but managed to persuade the chief steward to give them a different diet for a short test period. The king's food had probably been offered to idols, and the meat would not have been *kosher*, drained of the blood according to the law of Moses (cf. Hos. **9.**3). The steward was delighted to find that his charges did so well on a vegetarian diet. He drew their rations, and he and his family doubtless enjoyed them (16)!

Daniel's confidence was justified, and he and his friends passed their tests with honours (17–20). God had Daniel where He wanted him for a great many years, and the young man lived to see not only the arrival of further exiles from Judah in 597 and 586 B.C., but also the wonderful day when Cyrus captured Babylon and allowed the exiles to return if they wished. This is the significance of v. 21, but Daniel continued several years longer (e.g. **10**.1).

Learn to prove the power of God in small ways before the big tests come (Jer. 12.5; Acts 13.13; 15.37,38).

Daniel 2.1-24   The Lost Dream

Nebuchadnezzar was not yet king when he won the battle of Carchemish, but soon afterwards he was summoned home on the death of his father, followed by his prisoners. We should therefore have expected the events of this chapter to be at least in the third year, not the second year, of his reign (1, cf. **1**.5). But the Babylonians generally did not begin to count a king's reign until the New Year after his accession. Thus, putting together this date and the three years of **1**.5, we have; first year training—accession year of Nebuchadnezzar; second year training—first year of king; third year training—second year of king. The training need not have taken the whole of three years. The interpretation of the dream faced Daniel almost immediately after his test.

We cannot tell whether Nebuchadnezzar had really forgotten his dream, or whether he was trying out the skill of his wise men to see whether they could read what was in his mind. The wise men are here called *Chaldeans*, which at this date meant *Babylonians*. It is used in this sense in **1**.4; **5**.30; **9**.1, whereas in this chapter and in **3**.8 (possibly); **4**.7; **5**.7,11, it refers to a class of wise men, which became its regular use later. We note that the second use occurs in the Aramaic portions, which were probably translated later, except for vs. 2 and 4 here, where the word was probably put into the Hebrew to make the chapter consistent when the Aramaic version was attached to it (see Introduction). The original Hebrew may have had *galdu*, which occurs in Babylonian writings as a term for *astrologers*.

Nebuchadnezzar was childishly unreasonable in his demand, especially when he began to threaten his wise men with death if they could not tell the dream (8,9), and actually gave orders to kill them (12).

Although Daniel was a member of the group, he obviously kept himself aloof from their magic and astrology. Thus he had not gone in with them to the king (14,15). Now he handles the situation as a man of God. He goes in quietly to the king, and obtains an extension of time (16). Then he appeals to his friends to join him in prayer (18), and in answer God shows him both the dream and its meaning (19). Before he goes in to the king, he lifts up his heart in praise to God (20–23). It is good to see his concern for his colleagues; whatever he thinks of their methods (27), he knows they do not deserve the mad punishment that the king was ready to give.

Compare Daniel's song of praise with other passages in Scripture, such as Prov. 2.1–15; 1 Sam. 2.1–10; 1 Kings 3.5–14.

Daniel 2.25-49   The Interpretation of the Dream

Daniel assures the king that his discovery of the dream and its interpretation did not depend on his natural wisdom or on magic arts (26–30). He describes and interprets the features of the strange dream of the image, which symbolizes four successive world empires.

Babylon is the gold head. The breast and arms are the joint Medo-Persian empire, initiated by Cyrus. The belly and thighs are Greece, which became the dominant empire when Alexander the Great conquered Persia. The legs and feet are the Roman empire, embracing more scattered peoples than any of the others, but never able to marry them all together into perfect union (43), mixed, but ruthless (41,42).

In the days of the Roman empire a superhuman stone falls on the image (34), and all that had gone to form the four empires is broken and blown away (34,35,44,45). The stone goes on growing until it becomes the size of a mountain (35), and this is the Kingdom of God, which endures for ever (44).

A fair interpretation is that the first coming of Jesus Christ was the falling of the stone on the image. Since then the stone has been growing into a mountain, as the gospel has gone through the world, although the completion will not come before Christ returns again.

Although Daniel is rewarded by being made head of the college of wise men (48), there is no hint of his compromising by becoming a priest or magician. His influence for the true God must have made itself felt; and it may have been what he told the others about the promises of God that was handed down to those wise men who partially understood the message of the Star in the east (Matt. 2.1 ff.).

If, as many suppose, the *Book of Daniel* was really written about 150 B.C. to encourage Jewish resistance against the divine claims of Antiochus Epiphanes (4 syllables), it is strange that the writer makes Nebuchadnezzar offer an oblation and incense to Daniel, as though he were divine (46).

Study other pictures of the Messiah as the Stone, e.g. 1 Pet. 2.6–8; Luke 20.17,18. Note the marginal references in each case.

76

Daniel 3 The Golden Image

Nebuchadnezzar's image was probably of wood, plated with gold. It towered up to 90 feet, but this may have included the plinth, which narrowed to 9 feet at the base of the image itself. The Colossus of Rhodes stood 70 feet. Nelson's Column in Trafalgar Square, London, is 145 feet, and the actual statue of Nelson is 18 feet high on top of the column. The image was presumably of a god, and not of the king himself (12,18). The locality of Dura (1) is unknown.

It was customary to gather large numbers of officials for dedication ceremonies, as Middle East inscriptions show (3). Daniel's three friends were there as governors (2.49), but Daniel himself, as head of the wise men, was evidently exempt from attendance. The word 'satraps' (3) is Persian, not Babylonian, but, since Daniel lived on into the Persian period, he could naturally use the Persian equivalent of the Babylonian word for the head of a province; in any case this is in the Aramaic section, which was probably translated from the Hebrew in the Persian period.

The lyre, trigon, and harp, are stringed instruments, whose names in this passage are basically Greek. Musical instruments travel from country to country in the hands of traders and mercenaries, and Greek traders were in Asia Minor from the 7th century, and there were Greek mercenaries in the Babylonian army.

The three friends are quietly persistent to the end. They do not make any conditions with God; deliverance or martyrdom are equally in His hand (17,18). So they are thrown into the lime kiln furnace through the open door (26). Then a miracle happens. Not only are they unharmed, although the flames roaring out of the door burnt their warders to death, but the fire destroys the ropes that bound them without damaging their clothes. There is good evidence for fire-walking through trenches of glowing ashes without the feet being harmed, but there is no known natural explanation of what happened to the three here.

The intervention of God is confirmed by the presence of one whom Nebuchadnezzar realizes is a supernatural figure (25). We may well recognize Him as the Lord Jesus Christ in one of His pre-incarnation appearances (cf. Gen. 16.11–13; 18.1,2,22).

The fire reveals the presence of the Lord. Consider Acts 18.9,10; 2 Cor. 12.7–10.

Daniel 4.1-18 The Tree Dream

This is Nebuchadnezzar's second recorded dream, but this time the meaning is personal to himself. Secular records describe occasional dreams which kings have felt to be significant, e.g. Xerxes dreamed that he was crowned with an olive shoot, with branches that stretched over the world.

The chapter is a public decree by Nebuchadnezzar. Whereas in 3.28,29 he had sanctioned the worship of the God of Israel as an alternative to other gods, he now admits that there is a supreme God Most High, whom he himself must bow to, since this God is King of kings.

It is not surprising that v. 3 is strongly reminiscent of Psa. **145**.5, 13, for in talking to the king about the meaning of his dream, Daniel would certainly have brought out some of the Scriptures, and Psa. **145** is a magnificent hymn of God's rule and providence, which lingered in Nebuchadnezzar's memory.

It is significant that the king did not send immediately for Daniel (6–8), although he had been the only one able to interpret the first dream. No doubt he had an uneasy feeling that this dream had some moral meaning, and he knew that the God of Daniel tended to make severe moral demands. This is a common human failing. People with doubts will often persist in reading sceptical books, and in ignoring authors with sensible Christian answers: if there is no God and no Godward significance in sin, then one can ease up in the demands of life.

The dream is vividly described, and needs only brief notes. The 'watcher' (13,17) is one of the angels who are always watchful to see what God would have them do (Ezek. **1**.18; Rev. **4**.8; Zech. **4**.10). The 'band of iron' (15) is either for restraint (of a madman) or for preservation, so that the stump is not dug up. 'Seven times' (16) in this Book and in the *Revelation* represents seven definite periods fixed by God, possibly years.

The world envies the big man, but he is often a very uneasy man under the surface, especially where God is concerned. Mark 6.20; Acts 24.25.

Daniel 4.19-37   Humbled Greatness

Clearly Daniel was fond of the king, and was appalled at the prediction in the dream (19). At the same time he took the dream to be a warning from God rather than an absolutely fixed destiny. Thus he urges Nebuchadnezzar to set aside his typical oriental despotism, and be a simple benefactor to his people (27), ruling under God (26). Otherwise he will certainly suffer the fate of the tree in the dream.

For twelve months nothing happened. Then one day the king went up to the flat roof of the palace, probably the top terrace of the so-called Hanging Gardens, from which he could see over the city which he had built, and which a modern writer describes as 'a cosmopolitan city, the like of which has never existed since, with the exceptions of Rome and perhaps New York' (Schneider, *Babylon is Everywhere*). As he shouted for the glory of it, a sudden madness fell on him, giving him the awful hallucination of being turned into an animal. He no longer behaved as a man, but insisted on being turned out to pasture, presumably in one of the royal parks where no one would interfere with him (33).

From v. 33 we gather that he must have been in this state for at least a year, but v. 34 does not say that he was mad for seven years, as vs. 16 and 25 might suggest. Just as the 'beast-nature' had been under the surface previously, so now in the depths of his mind he was coming to terms with God and himself, and thus fulfilled the requirement of the end of v. 25.

Note how this section (28–33) is in the third person; Nebuchadnezzar could not describe exactly what was happening. With v. 34 we return to the confession, again paraphrasing Psa. **145**, and also bringing in something from Isa. **40**.22,26; **43**.13. Daniel would certainly have regarded these chapters of *Isaiah* as very precious, since they foretold the ultimate release from Babylon. In talking to the king (27), he would have found plenty of relevant passages about God's sovereignty there.

Secular records of Nebuchadnezzar's reign are incomplete, but a quotation from Megasthenes (about 300 B.C.) says that Nebuchadnezzar on the roof of his palace was suddenly possessed by a spirit, and, after foretelling the end of the Babylonian empire, suddenly disappeared. This could be a perverted version of the true account in this chapter.

1 Cor. 4.7 is God's corrective for boasting.

Daniel 5.1-16   The Writing on the Wall

Contemporary records say that Nabonidus, the last Babylonian king, 'entrusted the kingship to his son, Bel-shar-usur', while he himself retired to Arabia. Because his father was still the supreme ruler, Belshazzar in this chapter cannot promise a higher position than 'the third ruler in the kingdom' (7).

There are three references to Nebuchadnezzar as the 'father' of Belshazzar (2,11,18). It seems unlikely from the records that Belshazzar was descended from Nebuchadnezzar, but 'father' has several usages in ancient documents. Here it stands for 'predecessor on the throne', as in an Assyrian inscription, which describes Jehu as son of Omri, although in fact Jehu had murdered the last of Omri's line and usurped the throne (2 Kings **9,10**). The queen in

v. 10 is unlikely to be one of the wives of Belshazzar, who were already present at the feast (3). She could have been the widow of Nebuchadnezzar, who had died 23 years earlier.

The date now is 539 B.C. Cyrus the Persian is at the gates, but Belshazzar believes that Babylon is easily able to resist him. All the top people join in a dinner of bravado, in which temple cups and bowls are turned to vulgar use (3, cf. 2 Kings **24**.13; **25**.15; Jer. **27**.19–22), and the many idols of Babylon have their praises sung (4).

At this point the party is thrown into a panic by a mysterious hand which writes four words on the wall. We need not suppose that the words were in an unknown language, but they could not be read intelligently. It may be, however, that the letters were in an unusual script, and were mixed up in some way like an anagram in a crossword. The wise men could not make sense of it, but when news of the panic reached the apartments where the elderly ex-queen was living, she was happy to go in and remind the young man, whose father had murdered her grandson and taken the throne from him, of what his predecessor, her husband, had done. He had turned to Daniel for help. So once more God's servant is summoned to meet the crisis.

When the enemy is at the gates bravery is better than bravado, cf. Isa. 22.12–14; Eph. 6.10–18.

Daniel 5.17-31 Found Wanting

The first part of this section (17–23) needs no special comment, apart from noting the powerful conclusion of v. 23.

The meaning of the writing is not easy to follow without a note of explanation. The words are three weights, a mina, a shekel (which is one-sixtieth of a mina), and half minas (*parsin* is the plural of *peres;* Daniel gives the singular in his interpretation in v. 28). The names suggest other words, i.e. numbered, weighed, divided; and *peres* also sounds like the word for 'Persians', *Paras*. A modern parallel would be if the hand had written 'Pound, pound, three-penny bit, ˋand half sovereigns', and Daniel· were to interpret as 'God has pounded your kingdom; you are not worth one little bit, and your sovereignty will be shared between the enemy.'

Belshazzar accepted the reading, but had no idea that it was so near fulfilment. That night the troops of Cyrus entered the city. The historian Xenophon says that Cyrus diverted the river, and his troops entered Babylon at night during the celebration of a festival, and killed the king.

There is no archaeological reference to a king called Darius immediately after the fall of Babylon (31). We must therefore assume that this was an alternative name for one of three rulers. (*i*) Cyrus, who had a Median mother, and who is referred to by Nabonidus as king of the Medes. In 6.28 we can translate 'and' by 'even', as in 1 Chron. 5.26, which has 'Pul king of Assyria, *even* the spirit of Tilgath-pilneser', where the two names refer to the same man.

(*ii*) Gubaru, who was appointed governor of Babylon by Cyrus, and who exercised considerable power, even appointing governors.

(*iii*) Cyaxares, the uncle of Cyrus and king of Media. Xenophon suggests that Cyrus made him courtesy king over all his empire. Note that he 'received the kingdom' (31). The Jewish historian Josephus, who had access to writings now lost, says that Darius, 'who had another name among the Greeks', took Daniel to Media. Note that in 10.4 Daniel is by the Tigris, a branch of which rose in Media, and not by the Euphrates, which was Babylon's river.

There are difficulties in each of these identifications, but they are not greater than if we try to explain how the author invented a fictitious king, when he knew all about Cyrus.

Consider the implications of the end of v. 23 for ourselves today.

Daniel 6.1-15   Discipline of Prayer

In the Hebrew Bible 5.31 stands as the opening verse of this chapter. Daniel does not say that Darius captured Babylon, though, if he is the same as Cyrus, he does not deny it. If Josephus is correct, Daniel now writes about his new patron, who had taken him to Media, and who exerted considerable authority from there. Otherwise he is still in Babylon under Cyrus or Gubaru.

By now Daniel was over eighty, but his wisdom and dependability drew from his enemies the striking admission of vs. 4 and 5. Darius was more vulnerable, and was flattered to hear that for a month he should be treated as the only god in the country. The reference in v. 7 is clearly to this, and not to any simple request by one neighbour to another. He is induced to make a binding decree to this effect (8, cf. Esth. 1.19; 8.8).

In v. 10 we see the man of God at his best. He did not stage a special protest, or suddenly do what he had not done before, but simply behaved 'as he had done previously'. The opponents knew what to look for. Daniel opened his western-facing window, looking towards the Jerusalem that his eyes would never see, and there he poured out his heart to God (1 Kings 8.29,30,48; Pss. 5.7; 138.2; Jon. 2.7). This is one of the places in the Bible where a man of God finds it right to defy a decree which the king had no right to make (cf. Acts 5.29. Contrast Rom. 13.1,2).

The three times for prayer were probably the time when the morning burnt offering was offered, when the temple was standing; noon or the afternoon; and sunset, when the evening offering was made (cf. 9.21).

What is the value in regular times for prayer? Note Pss. 55.17; 119.164; 1 Chron. 23.30; Acts 3.1; 10.9,30.

Daniel 6.16-28   The Lions' Den

We have to decide from the brief description and from common-sense about the form of the den of lions. It cannot have been a dark pit with an entrance only at the top, since lions could neither be lowered into such a pit nor have been kept alive at the bottom. Since, as we saw in ch. 3, the three men were 'cast into' the furnace through an entrance at the side, Daniel was presumably cast into the den through a similar door. The lions would thus be in something like the bear pits at the zoo, though there may well have been a drop inside the door as an additional protection for the keepers (23,24).

It was already dark when Daniel was put in the den (14,15), so it was impossible to see down into the pit from the spectators' gallery at the top. The lower door was habitually closed with a stone, and this was now sealed so that no one could tamper with it during the hours of darkness (17). The king arrived before it was fully light in the morning (19), and called to Daniel before he actually reached the spot where he could look down into the den.

The cruel punishment of v. 24 is typically Persian. Obviously only the ringleaders are meant, and not all the satraps mentioned in v. 1.

The words of praise by Darius in vs. 26,27 are not, like Nebuchadnezzar's (4.3), reminiscent of a psalm, but spontaneously recognize the eternity of God's rule and His supreme power.

Concerning v. 28, if Darius is the same as Cyrus, we translate 'and' by 'even', as explained in note on 5.31. If he is Gubaru or Cyaxares, the reference here is to their joint rule.

Study the way in which Darius progressed in faith.

Questions for further study and discussion on Daniel chs. 1–6

1. What do these chapters teach about the need to stand for our principles? What sort of principles must we stand for?
2. How does the character of Daniel show a proper blend of humility and of complete confidence in God which made him bold?

82

3. What did Nebuchadnezzar, Belshazzar, and Darius learn through the witness of Daniel and his friends?
4. Find other passages in Scripture that speak of the Lord's deliverance in time of trouble, and also passages where He does not deliver. What then should be our attitude when trouble, or even death, threatens?

Daniel 7.1-18 God on the Throne

With this chapter we begin the description of the visions that God gave to Daniel. They are arranged in chronological order, this one being in 554 B.C., when Nabonidus gave the kingship of Babylon to his son.

The four kings (17) are the rulers of the four world empires that had already been depicted in Nebuchadnezzar's vision of the great image (ch. 2). This time they are symbolized by four wild animals.

(*i*) The lion (4) is Babylon, but more specifically. it symbolizes Nebuchadnezzar, Babylon's greatest king. His eagle wings were plucked when his madness humbled his flight in the face of heaven, but his subsequent confession of God's glory shows that he has the mind of a man, since a true man is one who admits his dependence on God.

(*ii*) The bear (5) is the Medo-Persian empire. The three ribs in its mouth probably have no special significance other than showing it to be a devouring beast. Its front paw, raised to slash, lifts its body on one side.

(*iii*) The leopard (6) is Greece, with Alexander the Great flying through Asia in his conquests. After his death his empire became four-headed, i.e. Asia Minor, Mesopotamia, Egypt, and Macedonia (cf. 8.8).

(*iv*) The terrifying beast, which is Rome, is only partially described (7). Its ten horns, like the ten toes of the image (2.41,42), are its federation of nations, loosely held together. We will leave the consideration of the little horn (8) until the next section.

Daniel, like some of the other prophets, was privileged to have a vision of God (9,10). He is impressed with His shining glorious brightness. This vision may be compared with Ezek. 1, together with the notes there. God is surrounded by the host of heaven. The picture is that of judgement, but probably not of the final judgement day. God's concern is the putting of the rule of the world into the hands of His Messiah. This is done by sending His Son into the Roman Empire, which had incorporated the earlier empires (12), and henceforth superseding it with His new kingdom (14).

If the scene is the final judgement, vs. 13, 14 must refer to the second coming. But in Matt. 26.64 Christ appears to be quoting these words of Himself, and says that the high priest will witness their fulfilment 'from now onwards'. This is the literal Greek, as indicated in the RV's 'henceforth'. Thus this vision begins with the ascension (Heb. 1.3,4; 10.12,13), although it runs through to completion at the second coming (cf. the stone becoming a mountain in 2.35).

Compare other visions of God, remembering that He can be seen only in a form that He chooses, and this must often be 'symbolic' (e.g. Exod. 24.17).

Daniel 7.19-28   Victory after Suffering

It is impossible to be dogmatic about the identity of the 'horn' in this passage. In chs. 8 and 11 Antiochus Epiphanes (4 syllables) is the persecutor, but the persecutor in this chapter is connected with the Roman Empire. The sequence here seems to be the coming of the Messiah in the time of the last of the single world empires, for, since Rome, world rule has been shared by various great powers at one and the same time.

Next comes violent persecution from the little horn, which rises in succession to other horns, and this persecution or war on the saints, continues until the final intervention by God. Some think that this is Antichrist, and, if he arises from Rome, there must be a revival of the Roman Empire still to come.

It is possible to take an intermediate view. Daniel is naturally concerned about the fate of his own people, the Jews. He does not know about the Christian Church, but the vision has the Church in mind, as well as the Jews. Thus Daniel sees a figure who was concerned both with the final destruction of the Jewish nation and also with launching the intense persecution of the Christians. This could be the Emperor Nero. Although he died before the destruction of Jerusalem in A.D. 70, it was he who sent Vespasian with the Roman armies to quell the Jewish rebellion. It was he also who organized the first big persecution of the Christians.

Nero himself did not exhaust the prophecy, any more than Antiochus exhausted other prophecies in *Daniel* (Matt. 24.15). He is like the beast in Rev. 13.3, whose head grows again when it is cut off. Thus the saints down the ages have had to face their Nero again and again, and there may be a final Nero in the person of Antichrist, even though there have been many antichrists (1 John 2.18).

We cannot give an explanation of the 'ten' and the 'three' in

v. 24. They may have reference to assassinations by Nero, or they may be general numbers, as we speak of 'dozens' and 'two or three': i.e. he will not be the first king of this empire, but there will be a number of others before him, and he will put down the few who oppose him.

Nero inaugurates wholesale persecutions of Christians and displays bitter hostility towards the true God; while he tries to force God's people to conform to his pattern (25; Rev. **13**.16,17). God's people have to submit to persecution for a specified time, known to God, whether days, weeks, months, or years (25). Yet through suffering we shall share in the victory of God, for Christ's kingdom is ours also (26,27).

Consider the relation between reigning with Christ (Eph. 2.6) and being persecuted for Christ's sake (2 Tim. 2.11–13).

*Daniel 8.1-12   Desecration

Daniel is visiting Susa, east of Babylon and south of Media, and is given a vision on the banks of the river Eulaeus. He sees a ram with two horns that denote Media and Persia (3,4,20). The taller horn is Persia, since Cyrus of Persia had conquered Media and absorbed it into his empire.

Next a goat comes from the west, and overthrows the ram. Greece conquers Persia (5-7,21). Alexander the Great is the goat's horn (5,21), and on his death his empire is divided between four other kings, who were in fact Alexander's generals (8,22). From one of them, Seleucus, who held the eastern part of the empire, another horn appeared after some 125 years (9,23). This was Antiochus Epiphanes, who came to the throne in 175 B.C.

He launches an attack on God, and begins by pulling down some of the stars and trampling on them (10). In the vision these probably represent the loyal people of God, who are put to death for their faith (24; **12**.3). Then he makes as direct an attack on God as he can, and desecrates the Temple in Jerusalem, forbidding the daily offering to be made on the altar (11,12). Historically Antiochus plundered the Temple and set up an altar to Zeus in the precincts, offering pig's flesh on it (168 or 167 B.C.).

The meaning of v. 12 may be that from among the people of God ('the host' as in vs. 10,11) there are those who become apostates, and so come under the sway of Antiochus when he takes control of the burnt offering. This links up with 'transgression'. Otherwise, it could be that loyal Jews are killed through the sin of Antiochus.

In what way can anyone attack God today?

This portion is more or less an interpretation of the vision, but there are several special features to note. In v. 14 we have one of several time-periods in *Daniel*. This one may have in mind the evening and morning sacrifices, which have been suspended by Antiochus. If so, the period is that of 2300 sacrifices, i.e. 1150 days. In actual fact the daily sacrifices were suspended for 1090 days, just over three years.

It is simpler to take the phrase, 'evenings and mornings', in the same sense as in Gen. 1.5, etc. Thus the period is the full 2300 days, and includes the time from the first interference in Jewish affairs in 171 B.C. to the death of Antiochus in 164 B.C.

In the vision Daniel hears a conversation between two angels (13), but the full interpretation comes from the angel Gabriel (16). The phrase, 'the time of the end' (17), must always be interpreted in the light of the context. It may refer to the end of a particular era as well as to the end of world history. There cannot be a reference to Antichrist here, since this vision does not even go as far as the 4th empire, Rome. Thus the 'end' cannot be the second coming. The persecutions by Antiochus were the last of the anti-God persecutions which might have destroyed the Jewish faith, before the coming of the Messiah, and it is in this sense that we may interpret 'the end'.

This time is also referred to as 'the latter end of the indignation', i.e. the conclusion of the persecuting rage of Antiochus and others (19). Daniel is assured that the worship in the Temple will once more be restored (14), and that the boasting Antiochus will die without achieving his aim of crushing the Jewish faith (25). In fact, Antiochus died of an illness, while planning fresh campaigns. The story of this period may be read in 1 Maccabees 1–6, in the Apocrypha.

Daniel is told to keep this record, but not to publish it until the time of the events (26; cf. **12.9**).

Somewhere today there is an Antiochus who is trying to stamp out the true faith. We know who will win, but let us pray especially for our brothers and sisters who are being trampled down.

●

Daniel 9.1-19   Confession of Sin

In 605 B.C. Nebuchadnezzar broke the power of Egypt at the battle of Carchemish. Egypt had to withdraw from Palestine, and the country came under the rule of Babylon. At this point Jeremiah foretold that the dominion of Babylon would last for seventy years, and would include the period of the exile (Jer. **25.**1–11). We noticed in ch. **4** that Daniel was familiar with the *Psalms* and *Isaiah*, and here we find him equally familiar with the prophecies of Jeremiah, some of which at least were already being incorporated into the collection of writings recognized as inspired (2).

It is now 538 B.C., approximately seventy years since the Jews came under Babylon (2), and Daniel is naturally anxious for the promised return to come as soon as possible. But he knows that the purpose of the exile was to prepare a repentant nucleus for the future. Hence he takes the lead in this prayer of confession of national sin.

Note the balance and contrast between the sin of the people and the righteousness of God, and between unfaithfulness and faithfulness (4–10). Daniel has also studied the Law of Moses, and admits that God had given full warning and promise in Lev. **26** and Deut. **28–30** (13,14).

He makes his final plea for restoration on the ground of the covenant (implied in v. 15) and for the sake of God's own great Name (17–19). So must we also pray in the Name of the Lord Jesus Christ.

Daniel's prayer embraced all of God's people, both the exiles whom he knew, and also those who were still living in Palestine, near Jerusalem (7). Prayer can easily be too local.

*It is worth comparing this prayer with Ezra **9** and Neh. **9**.*

Daniel 9.20-27   The Messiah

Daniel included himself in his prayer of confession (20). It is dangerous to be critical of others in our prayers without considering ourselves. He had been thinking only of an immediate return from exile, and God was quick to answer his prayer, since almost immediately Cyrus gave permission to the Jews to return (Ezra **1**). But just as Isaiah was shown in chs. **40–55** that there would not only be a return from Babylon, but also a return from the exile of sin through the atoning work of God's Servant (especially ch. **53**), so Daniel is shown that the climax of Jewish history is not only the return, but the subsequent coming of the Messiah, and that there is a second time-scale for Jeremiah's words. The interpreter is appropriately the same Gabriel who later announced to the virgin Mary that she would be the mother of the Messiah (21; Luke **1**.26 ff.).

In this commentary we have room for only one interpretation of the figures and statements in vs. 24–27. The finished work of Christ is described in v. 24. The first four clauses are obvious. 'To seal both vision and prophet' means to set God's seal of fulfilment on the Messianic prophecies of the O.T. 'To anoint a most holy place' is better taken as in the margin of 'a most Holy One', i.e. Christ.

Certain periods are mentioned on a scale of a year for a day (24). In prophecy a year is 360 days, or 12 months of 30 days each (Rev. 11.2,3). The only recorded command to rebuild Jerusalem (25) is in Neh. 2.1 ff., i.e. 446 B.C. In v. 25 the AV and RV margin transliterate 'an anointed one' as 'the Messiah', assuming, probably correctly, that by this time the word was already beginning to be the title of the One who should come.

We are also free to follow the AV and RV margin again with the figures, and punctuate, 'there shall be seven weeks and sixty-two weeks; it shall be built again', i.e. the city will be built, and the Messiah will come after 69 weeks of years, which are 483 years of 360 days, or 476 years, according to our chronology. From 446 B.C. the 476 years would end in A.D. 30, which could be the start of Christ's ministry as Minister of the New Covenant for His people. We thus take the first half of v. 27 as referring to Christ, whose death, when He was cut off after about half a week (3 to $3\frac{1}{2}$ years), ended the Jewish sacrifices. The week ends with the death of Stephen and the opening of the doors to the Gentiles.

His rejection by the nation as a whole resulted in the destruction of Jerusalem by the Romans in A.D. 70 (26,27, cf. Matt. 23.29–39). The final word of v. 27 may be translated 'desolate' (RV margin). The Romans will fly upon the city and bring about the ultimate pollution of the Temple and the scattering of the ruined nation.

Consider v. 24 in the light of Heb. 10.1–22.

Daniel 10.1—11.1 War in Heaven

Daniel has a vision of a conflict (1) which concerns heaven as well as earth. He has been keeping the Passover and Feast of Unleavened Bread, as the date in v. 4 shows, but his private fasting and prayer had lasted longer than the stipulated week (2). He is rewarded by a vision of a glorious being (5,6), who may be Christ Himself (Rev. 1.13–15), but who might be Gabriel or some other angel. V. 7 may be compared with what happened at Paul's conversion (Acts 9.7).

Vs. 12–21 are an O.T. equivalent of what Paul says in Eph. 6.10–18 about the heavenly warfare. It is clear that an evil angel can dominate a nation (13,20), and that there is some power equivalent to a national guardian angel. Michael is spoken of in these terms as the angel who stands behind Israel (13,21; 12.1). The Seventh Day Adventists hold that Michael is the pre-incarnate title of Christ, and this is possible, provided that we also accept His deity, as the Adventists do. Jehovah's Witnesses reject His deity, though they believe that He was Michael and a created being.

The speaker, or speakers, in this chapter speak of the way God had used them and would use them again in the events of history. Note that in **11.1** 'him' is Michael and not Darius.

Consider our warfare in the light of Eph. 6.12,13 and Col. 2.15.

Daniel 11.2-28 The Plan of History

In this chapter we have a most detailed prediction of the course of history. We ourselves would like to see more predictions of our own day, but it was important for the Jewish nation that God should prepare them to face one of the strongest attempts that would ever be made to force them to apostatize. It would be the final attempt before the coming of the Messiah.

The next three kings of Persia (2) were Cambyses, Gaumata, and Darius I. Darius campaigned unsuccessfully against Greece, and his son, Xerxes I, launched a further big attack (3). He also was defeated in 480 B.C. This is the Xerxes of the book of *Esther*. The prophecy now passes to the Greek conquest of Persia under Alexander the Great in 334–330 B.C. (3), though his empire was divided among four of his generals on his death (4).

Ptolemy I ruled Egypt. Seleucus, who had been allotted Babylonia, was forced to escape to Egypt, and served as one of Ptolemy's generals until he could get his kingdom back. Eventually this kingdom stretched from Palestine to India (5). Some fifty years later Ptolemy II gave his daughter in marriage to Antiochus I, a Seleucid, but Antiochus deserted her, and himself was murdered (6). Her brother, Ptolemy III, invaded Syria in 246 B.C. (7,8).

Vs. 9–13 describe the see-saw struggles between the Seleucids of Syria and the Ptolemies of Egypt between 223 B.C. and about 200 B.C. At this point some of the Jews joined in with Antiochus III of Syria, imagining that they were fulfilling some prophecy (14). The Egyptian army was besieged and defeated in Sidon (15), and Antiochus broke the hold of Egypt on Palestine (16). He came to terms with Ptolemy V, and gave him his daughter in marriage, hoping that this would turn out to his own advantage (17). Antiochus III then annexed the coastlands of Asia Minor, and even invaded Greece, but here he was defeated by a Roman commander, and forced to withdraw (18). The Romans followed him, defeated him at Magnesia in 190 B.C., and forced him to pay heavy tribute. He died shortly afterwards (19).

His son, Seleucus IV, exacted tribute from the Jews and others in order to pay the Romans, but he was poisoned not long after an attempt by his agent to seize the Temple treasures (20). His brother, Antiochus IV, known as Epiphanes, succeeded him, and became the great persecutor. By personal influence he managed to be chosen king in place of the son of Seleucus (21). Vs. 22–24 give a sketch of his character and way of life. He despised covenants and alliances, but got his way through a small body of supporters, plundering one area to bribe another.

In 173 B.C. Antiochus defeated Ptolemy VI, captured him, and was crowned as king of Egypt. Some of Ptolemy's courtiers turned traitor (25,26). When the Egyptians set up the brother of Ptolemy VI as king, Antiochus made a half-hearted attempt to restore Ptolemy VI, but this was unsuccessful (27). He therefore retired to Syria, but planned to attack the Jews (28).

These verses have been given contemporary interpretations at various times. Consider how far this is due to invariable factors that lead men to alliances and wars.

Daniel 11.29-45 The End of the Persecutor

Antiochus again invaded Egypt (29), but Roman ambassadors, arriving by ship, forced him to withdraw (30). The Jews were quarrelling over the high priesthood, and the liberal group were glad to have his help (30). However, Antiochus did not rest until he had totally profaned the Temple and its worship (31; see notes on 8.1–12). A number of Jews stood firm, in spite of torture and martyrdom (32,33). They received support from the militant Maccabees, who became powerful enough to frighten some half-hearted Jews into giving nominal support (34). Moreover, in time of persecution even the genuine believers are stimulated to greater devotion (35).

Antiochus had coins struck describing himself as THEOS EPIPHANES (God Manifest) (36), and set aside the traditional gods, including Apollo and Tammuz (or Adonis, the darling god of women) (37), and set up a temple to Jupiter Capitolinus in Antioch (38), and acknowledged him as his guardian (39).

Vs. 40–45 have given rise to various interpretations. They do not describe what actually happened towards the end of Antiochus' life. There are three main lines of interpretation.

(*i*) Antiochus is a type of Antichrist, and in these verses we jump to an attack on the Holy Land before the final coming of Christ.

(*ii*) Since in this chapter there have been various kings of the south and the north, we now have the end of the Syrian empire, when a new king of the north, i.e. Rome under Crassus, subdues the former king, pillages the Temple (54 B.C.), and takes over

90

Palestine. However, in a war against the Parthians of the north-east, Crassus is killed (44,45).

(*iii*) These verses contain a summary of Antiochus' actions during his whole career, just as vs. 36–39 contain a summary of his methods. He was successful almost everywhere, even apparently against God and His people and holy Temple. Only the Parthians in the north-east remained as a threat (44). The last sentence of the chapter does not say that he died in Palestine. He set himself up as God, but he died like an ordinary man. His death in Persia in 164 B.C. (or 163) was sudden and unexpected. This was the end of the pre-Messianic persecutions, and from now onwards the Roman empire was beginning to take over world power.

Death is the great humiliator. Pss. 49.16–20; 82.6,7; Luke 12.20.

Daniel 12.1-6   Sifting

There is so much to consider in this final chapter, that we divide it into two short portions.

If Antichrist is the subject of the closing verses of the previous chapter, the opening verses here refer to the time of the Lord's return. If, however, Antiochus has been the subject, we have come to the end of the great persecution on account of faith; the Greek empire has given place to the early domination by Rome, which gave the Jews considerable freedom. Now the Jewish nation is to be sifted once again when confronted by the promised Messiah.

The intervention of Michael (1) is then the throwing down of Satan as recorded in Rev. 12.7–12. This victory over Satan is linked with the efficacy of the death of Jesus Christ (Rev. 12.11; John 12.31f.). But for the Jewish nation as a whole, their clinging to nationalism and rejection of the Messiah led to their scattering and tribulation (Luke 21.20–24). However, many among the Jews will accept the Messiah and their names are in the Book of Life (1). If we do not take v. 1 to refer to some special period of trouble shortly before the Lord returns, the meaning is that the continuing sufferings that the Jewish nation has undergone up to the present day are unique in history.

In the reference to the resurrections in v. 2, still to come, it is not clear why the words speak of 'many' rather than 'all'. Probably the verse is singling out Daniel's nation, who are many; it ignores the Gentile dead. Even among God's chosen people there are both sheep and goats.

V. 3 has meant much to many people who are concerned with witness for God by life and speech (cf. 11.33,35; 12.10). Meanwhile Daniel has to keep what he has written, and not disclose it publicly.

During the last persecutions before the Messiah's coming, those who have the book will make it known (cf. Rev. 22.10). Although it is tempting to apply the closing sentence of v. 4 to the present day, it is more likely that it means that many will run to study the book in order to increase their knowledge of God (cf. Amos 8.12; Hab. 2.2).

Compare v. 3 with Mal. 3.16–4.3; Phil. 2.15,16. We do well to examine ourselves.

Daniel 12.7-13 The End

This remarkable book ends with figures and dates that are not easy to decipher. One at least is either absolutely literal or else the most curious coincidence in history. This is the figure in v. 12 of 1335 days. General Allenby captured Jerusalem in the year 1335, according to the Muslim calendar, which was the one used by the Turks who at that time held Jerusalem. This was 1917 in our era, and marked the first step in the liberation of Israel's land.

The other dates are not so clear, unless we throw everything into the future in connection with the events accompanying the second coming. The period of 'a time, two times, and half a time' (7; cf. 7.25) may indicate a literal 3½ years, but since the words that follow, apparently referring to the same period, are general, it may be that the phrase indicates that it will be for a definite period, not known to man, but prescribed by God. (See note on 7.25.)

The reference in v. 11 is to Antiochus, who stopped the daily sacrifices, so v. 7 may also refer to him. As explained in the note on 8.14, the actual desecration lasted for 1090 days (3 years and 10 days). It is reasonable to suppose that the period of 1290 years is the time from the desecration to the death of Antiochus. He died in the same year as the Temple was cleansed, but we do not know how long afterwards.

There is a wider application of v. 10 than to the book of *Daniel* alone. Christ and the Bible are the source both of ultimate wisdom, and of confusion to those who are not prepared to consider their accountability to God (1 Cor. 2.6–16; 2 Cor. 2.15,16). But Daniel would not have us be content with wisdom alone, for God's wisdom is given to lead us to purity (10; 1 John 3.2). Daniel himself sets us this example in his book, and it is a happy thought that we shall share with him in Christ's glorious resurrection (13). Meanwhile we, the people of God, still suffer, and we look for the time of the end when Christ returns. But we stand on the victory side of the cross, which Daniel saw by faith. Christ has broken into history that history which Daniel saw sketched out briefly beforehand

and by a real incarnation, atoning death, resurrection, and ascension, He has wrought our redemption, given us new life, and founded His Kingdom that will supersede all other limited kingdoms, and, unlike the others, will never pass away.

Think out the link between wisdom and purity of life.

Questions for discussion and further study on Daniel chs. 7–12

1. Which passages in the Book indicate that Daniel was told something of the incarnation, atoning death, and enthronement (which would, of course, imply resurrection) of Jesus Christ?
2. Why are the empires depicted as animals?
3. What functions do angels fulfil in the plan of God (e.g. Heb. 1.14)?
4. How far does prediction relieve us of responsibility for our actions (e.g. Matt. 26.24)?